Forbes
Numbers Game

That's a Lot of GAAP and other accounting
controversies from the Editors of FORBES

Edited and with an Introduction by

Lawrence Minard

Associate Editor, Forbes Magazine

and

David A. Wilson

Arthur Young & Company, Houston

Prentice-Hall, Inc., Englewood Cliffs, New Jersey 07632

Library of Congress Cataloging in Publication Data

Main entry under title:

Forbes Numbers Game.

    "Anthology of 34 Forbes 'The Numbers Game' articles."
    Includes Index.
      1. Accounting–Addresses, essays, lectures.
I.   Minard, Lawrence.   II.   Wilson, David A., 1941-
III.   Forbes magazine
HF5635.F73   657   79-27484
ISBN 0-13-325100-4

Editorial/production supervision
and interior design by **Esther S. Koehn**
Cover by **Jerry Pfiefer**
Manufacturing buyer: **Edmund W. Leone**

Printed in the United States of America

10   9   8   7   6   5   4   3   2   1

Prentice-Hall International, Inc., *London*
Prentice-Hall of Australia Pty. Limited, *Sydney*
Prentice-Hall of Canada, Ltd., *Toronto*
Prentice-Hall of India Private Limited, *New Delhi*
Prentice-Hall of Japan, Inc., *Tokyo*
Prentice-Hall of Southeast Asia Pte. Ltd., *Singapore*
Whitehall Books Limited, Wellington, *New Zealand*

Acknowledgments

Above all else, this book owes its existence to Malcolm Forbes, proprietor and editor-in-chief of FORBES magazine, who very generously gave us permission to reprint these articles, all of which appeared originally in his magazine; to FORBES Senior Editor Geoffrey Smith who helped create "The Numbers Game" column in the first place; and to James Michaels, editor of FORBES, who has encouraged his writers to write the column and who encouraged us in preparing this anthology.

Lawrence Minard dedicates this book to Ruth and Larry Norton for their unflagging inspiration.

David Wilson dedicates the book to Marsha, Bennett and Sean.

Contents

Introduction

As readers of FORBES magazine know, the theory and practice and social status of accounting are far different today from what they were 75, 50, or even 15 years ago. In simpler times mighty American industrialists and financiers could run their empires pretty much as they pleased, with no accountants looking over their shoulders. Financial statements were little more than personal notebooks that could be carried around in a waistcoat pocket. Financial disclosure? Auditor's opinions? Generally Accepted Accounting Principles? These were topics that concerned a tiny portion of the public—a handful of New York or European bankers here, a wealthy Boston or Chicago shareholder there. If the wider public thought about accountants at all, it thought of colorless men endowed with powers of addition and subtraction and not much else.

For a flavor of the accountant's status in a simpler age, consider this acid stereotype from turn-of-the-century American folk philosopher Elbert Hubbard:

> The typical auditor is a man past middle age, spare, wrinkled, intelligent, cold, passive, noncommittal, with eyes like a codfish, polite in contact, but at the same time, unresponsive, cold, calm and damnably composed as a concrete post or plaster-of-Paris cast; a human petrification with a heart of feldspar and without charm of the friendly germ, minus bowels, passion, or a sense of humor. Happily, they never reproduce and all of them finally go to hell.

Accounting was obviously not a trade worthy of bright and eager young men—and even less so for women.

Today, of course, the accountant's lot is altogether different. Hubbard's stereotype is crumbling on all sides. The modern accountant is as far removed from his uninspiring predecessor in a green eyeshade and celluloid shirtcuff as the modern neurosurgeon is removed from a dusty country physician with his battered black bag. Accounting is now highly controversial and very much in the news.

"SEC's Ability to Act Against Accountants Is Backed by Court In Case Against Touche Ross," blared a recent *Wall Street Journal* headline.

"Chemical Bank Sues 3 Frigitemp Ex-Aids, Arthur Andersen & Co.," read a *Journal* headline the next day.

"Measure Allowing Challenges to Mergers of Big Partnerships Clears Senate Panel," said a headline of the third day, referring to big law and accounting firm mergers.

And so it goes. As Donald Sloan, managing partner of international accounting firm Peat Marwick Mitchell's New York office recently summed it up: "The public, and in particular government agencies, are demanding that auditors become policemen of corporate managements, not just on matters of corporate fraud, but in a host of new areas ranging from overseas bribery to executive lunches. Auditors are beginning to audit other auditors, with special panels to audit the audits of auditors. We are being asked to fathom the future, or what is probably worse, to certify that our clients have correctly done so. In short, we risk becoming philosophers and astrologers and guardians of public mortality—with full legal liability if we trip up."*

The risk is not without its reward, of course. The once-lowly accountant is now near the top of America's economic elite. "Would You Like Your Daughter To Marry An Accountant (Or To Become One)?" asked the headline of a recent FORBES magazine cover story on the impressive economics of the accounting profession. The headline continued: "Read This Article Before You Answer In The Negative," and the article went on to report that America's 400,000-odd accountants now outearn, on average, the U.S.'s 200,000-odd lawyers—and that partners at the top accounting firms routinely earn upwards, often well in excess of $100,000 annually.** In this context, it is not surprising to hear Professor Anelise N. Mosich, then chairman of the University of Southern California's Accounting Department report:

> Suddenly students see accounting as glamorous, sexy. Many of our best students, who would have gone to law school a couple of years ago, are now going into public accounting.

For over a decade, FORBES magazine has regularly reported the sea-changes rocking the accounting profession. It is only natural that FORBES'

---

*The New Accountant—The Myth and the Reality," *The CPA Journal,* February 17, 1978.
**"The U.S.' Newest Glamour Job," FORBES, September 1, 1977.

editors should pay such attention to accounting. The magazine's 1.7-million readers are sophisticated businessmen and women whose daily professional decisions are in large measure based upon financial facts and figures categorized, certified, and disclosed by accountants. And to investigate and judge the companies and governments they write about, FORBES' writers are confronted daily with making sense of reams of accounting rules, annual reports, quarterly reports and the like that seem to grow fatter and more complex each year.

Perceiving early on and from first-hand experience the new demands being made of accountants (and remembering Benjamin Disraeli's great one-liner: "There are lies, damn lies, and statistics"), FORBES' Editor James Michaels and Senior Editor Geoffrey Smith created a special feature column to track what was shaping up as a real revolution in accounting. The year was 1973. The action was fast and getting faster. The old Accounting Principles Board was crumbling, and the new Financial Accounting Standards Board was scheduling its first meetings when Michaels introduced the new column in these words:

> With this issue a new FORBES feature is born. Entitled "The Numbers Game," it tackles, in what we hope is a bright and interesting fashion, that traditionally dry-as-dust subject, financial accounting. The first column demonstrates how—deliberately or otherwise—Ampex Corp. and its auditors may have misled investors in its 1972 annual report. Through the column we hope to help readers learn more about what to look for in the fine print of corporate reporting. A little immodestly perhaps, we also hope that through intelligent critism—not shrill carping— we may even contribute to raising the standards of financial reporting . . .

That was in July 1973. Since then, nearly 100 "Numbers Game" articles have appeared and the feature has become one of FORBES' most popular—and influential. It is read regularly by the accounting rule-makers; individual articles were introduced to the late Senator Lee Metcalf's landmark investigation of whether the Federal Government should write accounting standards and generally regulate what Metcalf called "The Accounting Establishment." Most important, however, the articles have amply demonstrated that the heated debates behind the accounting principles themselves are often far more relevant to understanding financial statements than the antiseptic annual and quarterly reports investors receive in the mail.

This book is the anthology of 34 FORBES' "The Numbers Game" articles. We think it will interest businessmen, investors, and practicing accountants who may have missed some of the articles when they were first published, or who want a convenient single volume reference source. Our primary audience, however, is students—undergraduate and graduate alike—enrolled in accounting and business administration programs, and perhaps law and business journalism courses as well. To them and their teachers we offer this collection as a supplementary book of readings to complement and amplify standard accounting textbooks, in hopes that we might, as FORBES' Jim Michaels put it, "contribute to raising the standards of financial reporting."

The topics covered in these "Numbers Games" are as diverse as the interests of FORBES' readers and editors. You will find here articles on professional sports franchise accounting, motion picture accounting, accounting for the costs of oil companies "dry holes" (wells with nothing in them), how-to accounting for foreign exchange rate fluctuations, whether and how to account for the ravages of inflation. It's a long menu. But varied as these articles are, they are tied together by such consistently raised questions as: Why does this *matter*? Which side of the argument is *right*, or more right? How *should* an accounting principle be *changed* for the better?

The FORBES' writers responsible for these articles have answered these questions as they saw fit when they wrote. But don't be satisfied with their answers. The hallmark of accounting today is relentless controversy and change. In this environment there are few "right" answers and "wrong" answers. Instead, there are well-argued answers and poorly argued ones. The editors of FORBES and the editors of this book hope that, at the very least, these articles will spur the level of debate on to higher levels.

A few words of warning: Many "Numbers Games" center on specific accounting principles constantly subject to change. As James Kerkley, the articulate executive vice-president of Monsanto Company, put it: "It must be remembered that accounting standards are nothing more than conventions developed over time. They represent an implicit agreement as to what information is useful in a financial statement." Over time, the implicit agreements change and with them, the standards change. Are these articles, then, in danger of being made obsolete? Will the controversies raised by them be resolved? Are you wasting your money buying this book?

We think not. The uncomfortable fact is, accounting's easy problems have already been solved. It is the really difficult questions that remain and around which the coming controversies will probably swirl. To understand and enter confidently into these controversies will require a sense of where the debates have already gone—Down which blind alleys? Down which promising ones? It's a funny thing about fundamental problems: The same themes appear over and again; a solution rejected this year will likely be re-presented a year or two hence. Thus does accounting seem more akin to philosophy than arithmetic.

Take, for example, the question of how oil companies should account for their dry-hole drilling expenses. "Numbers Games" on this topic appear on page 70. The debate over the successful-efforts accounting method and the full-cost method has raged for several years. In 1978, the Financial Accounting Standards Board "solved" the problem by ordering all firms to use only the successful-efforts method. But only a few months later, the Securities and Exchange Commission overrode the FASB and told oil companies to begin using something called "reserve recognition accounting"—an entirely new accounting approach for the companies.

End of debate? Not so fast. Today there is considerable doubt that the SEC's method, which seems very reasonable in theory, can be put into meaningful practice. (When you read "You can't legislate accounting principles!" on page 74, you'll wonder too.) If it cannot be, then the debate will start anew, and the first "Numbers Game" addressing the controversy will seem as fresh as when first published—which was in 1973!

Or take inflation accounting, which rates an entire section in this anthology. (It starts at page 79.) Nearly everyone today agrees that reported corporate profits have been rendered next to meaningless by persistent worldwide inflation. Trouble is, most of today's accounting principles rest upon historical-cost accounting. So what are the accounting rule-makers to do? Scrap the entire historical-cost framework and create an entirely new foundation? Or limp along with modifications to the old, admittedly inadequate rules? As with dry-hole accounting, you'll be better able to follow and join in the coming debates over inflation accounting after reading the "Numbers Game" devoted to this pressing problem.

In fact, we have tried to select for this collection especially those "Numbers Game" articles that go directly to the fundamental questions that matter to FORBES' readers. When is an asset really an asset? Of what do liabilities really consist? When is a debt a short-term liability and when is it long-term? Do the rules underlying Generally Accepted Accounting Principles themselves deserve general acceptance? The sort of question that can save you a lot of money if you're an investor, perhaps save you a lawsuit if you're an accountant (or start one for you if you're a lawyer), and by all means stimulate heated classroom debate if you're a student.

When you read these articles, then, keep in mind that they were written by FORBES' journalists as news articles. Each article has its own historical context; we have appended original publication dates and, where especially necessary, epilogues to the ends of these collected articles.

But keep this in mind, too: The basic controversies die hard, and for better or worse accounting today is riddled with basic controversies. If it weren't accountants today would probably still suffer the low esteem ascribed to them by Elbert Hubbard three-quarters of a century ago.

In preparing this volume, our overriding debt is to Malcolm Forbes and Jim Michaels. We also want to thank the FORBES writers who wrote the "Numbers Game" column, in particular: Geoffrey Smith, Subrata Chakravarty, Steve Forbes, James Flanigan, Howard Rudnitsky, Paul Blustein, Brian McGlynn,

and Paul Sturm. We also hope that the students and teachers—and all others—
who use this book will tell us, frankly, what they think of it, so that future
editions may profit.

> Lawrence Minard
> London, England

> David A. Wilson
> Houston, Texas

July 19, 1979

1

THAT'S A LOT OF GAAP!

> In our opinion, the statements mentioned above present fairly the consolidated financial position of the corporation. . . in conformity with generally accepted accounting principles applied on a consistent basis during the period.

So runs the letter accountants write whenever they issue an opinion on the financial statements of a corporation. It is an august phrase, one that suggests high objectivity and scientific training. Until recently bankers and lawyers, businessmen and investors, widows and orphans felt they could sleep easily on financial statements presented in conformity with Generally Accepted Accounting Principles or GAAP. Increasingly, however, users of financial statements are asking: Just what stands behind those august words?

What stands behind GAAP? That is not an easy question as the articles in *Forbes Numbers Game* repeatedly demonstrate. These readings, most of them anyway, show that many of accounting's seemingly most cherished, most solid rules and concepts are in fact subject to heated debate between businessmen and accountants, between politicians and accountants—and between *accountants* and accountants. Today's accounting rules and concepts are certainly superior to no rules or concepts at all. But they are far less objective and scientific than most users of financial statements probably think. They may even be misleading. This is why those august opinions must never be relied upon blindly. We think *Forbes Numbers Game* selections will make that point over and again.

Sports writers would never attempt to evaluate, say, baseball without first agreeing that the rules by which the game is played are appropriate and adequate. So with us. We begin this anthology with a piece that asks: How good is the body of generally accepted accounting principles, GAAP, the rules by which the accounting game is played? Not very good, the article says. But we urge you not to form a premature opinion. Read the rest of the selections in this book—or skip ahead to the concluding two readings, which return to the fundamental question of GAAP's adequacy—before judging GAAP. Then make up your own mind.

"That's a lot of GAAP!"

Here's a one question quiz that could save you some money.

True or false: When outside auditors certify that a company's financial statements "present fairly the financial position" of the company, the investor has a guarantee that the books fairly present the financial reality.

Sad though it be, the statement is false. When you see the "presents fairly" phrase, the accountants are confirming no more than that the financial statements are "in conformity with generally accepted accounting principles." Thus the books of U.S. Financial, Penn Central, National Student Marketing, Equity Funding, and many more, all "presented fairly."

As Securities & Exchange Commissioner A.A. Sommer says: "The application of GAAP does not guarantee there will be a fair presentation."

Are you a bit confused at this point? We don't blame you. How can "presents fairly" be anything other than a fair presentation? Putting aside semantics, we can best illustrate with an example.

Remember Stirling Homex? It was going to do for housing what Henry Ford once did for cars. But only insiders got rich. Just 29 months after going public, Stirling Homex folded, leaving the investing public shortchanged by an estimated $100 million. Believe it or not, Stirling Homex' statements were stamped "presents fairly" and by no less an accounting firm than Peat Marwick Mitchell.

We dusted off Stirling's July 31, 1971 annual report—its last. Everything looked fine. Sales and earnings were up 63 percent and 60 percent respectively. Working capital from operations more than doubled and shareholders' equity tripled. Wall Street was paying 250 times earnings for the stock.

The only hint of trouble was on the balance sheet. Current liabilities—mainly unsecured bank notes—nearly tripled, to $46 million.

But that hint of gloom was obscured by Peat Marwick's certification letter. It clearly stated that Stirling Homex' statements ". . .present fairly the consolidated financial position of Stirling Homex . . . in conformity with generally accepted accounting principles. . ."

Yet only 12 months later, the company was in receivership.

How can "presents fairly" present so unfairly?

The accountants mostly insist upon judging "fairness" in terms of an established framework of rules—generally accepted accounting principles. If a company's accounting policies conform to generally accepted accounting principles, the results automatically yield a fair presentation. "That makes the accountant's life easy," explains John Shank, associate professor of accounting and finance at the Harvard Business School, "because then the accountant doesn't have to apply any independent judgment to the situation. He only has to decide whether his judgment conforms to the rules." That's like following a cake recipe and worrying only about counting cups of flour—not about how it's finally going to taste.

Accruing Trouble

The secret to Stirling Homex' rosy sales and earnings picture was a modern accounting concept known as "accrual accounting," which attempts to match income with expense. The minute a house rolled off the assembly line, Stirling Homex rang up a sale based on purported purchase contracts, even though the cash was a long way from the company till. The SEC charges 85.8 percent of Stirling Homex' 1971 sales were improperly recorded. But if you use accrual accounting the way Stirling Homex did, its numbers were "presented fairly."

To resolve the fair presentation problem, Commissioner Sommer and Chief Accountant John C. (Sandy) Burton of the SEC have recently urged accountants to take a broader approach to the phrase. Burton argues that GAAP is not the *only* important aspect of fairness. He suggests that GAAP rules should be part of a broad "accounting model" before the accountant approves a company's report. Accountants should realize they are talking to investors, not just to other accountants, and they must be responsible for making subjective judgments as to the overall fairness of the picture painted by corporate financial statements. As Sandy Burton puts it, accountants should be asking, "What is the *reality* behind a particular transaction?"

In the case of Stirling Homex, for example, this approach might have encouraged Peat Marwick accountants to ask some tougher questions. Questions like: "Where is the cash behind those sales, *really?*" Or even: "What *really* are the financial foundations of this company?"

If you want to make an accountant squirm, just suggest that this is the way it should be done. They have good reason to squirm. It would take them away from rules with which they feel safe and comfortable and throw them into a whole new world of subjective judgments—and, of course, of risk. For one thing, it would open up the possibility of getting into an argument with a good customer. He may want to handle a transaction in a certain way—as Stirling Homex did with accrual sales. Is the accountant then to append a note to his report suggesting that the client is hiding something? Hardly a way to keep the client happy.

And then, of course, there are the lawyers. Once judgment rather than fairly rigid rules enters into the picture, so does the possibility of lawsuits against the accountants. As Peat Marwick's general counsel, Victor Earle III, puts it: "It's fine to talk about fairness and motherhood and all that. But what happens when a jury determines liability if they're allowed to do so on the basis of *their* view of fairness? What I don't want is a standard of liability that says even where the accountant in good faith followed all the accounting requirements and touched all the bases, he's still liable if the layman doesn't think his presentation was fair."

Earle is uncomfortably aware that the accountants are already seriously exposed.

Starting with the landmark Continental Vending case of 1969, the courts have, in most observers' opionions, consistently held that compliance with GAAP is not in itself a complete defense. According to the courts, when push comes to shove, the accountants *are* responsible for an overall fair presentation.

Real Tiger

Why all the fuss? Haven't most of the abuses been ended? Not necessarily. Many of the old GAAP-sanctioned practices that have led to abuses in the past are still available to the clever entrepreneur. Accrual accounting is just one of the ways reality can be distorted. Pooling—the simple addition of balance sheet items in the case of mergers—is another. It was pooling that allowed International Telephone & Telegraph to boost its pretax earnings from 1970 to mid-1974 by nearly $240 million, after its merger with Hartford Fire. According to pooling critics, the gain was illusory. According to GAAP, it was legitimate. And as recent Numbers Games have demonstrated, GAAP practices governing foreign currency translations and gains from early extinguishment of debt are still potentially misleading.

As John Shank says: "No matter how detailed the accounting rules, the mind of the enterprising entrepreneur can always conceive of a transaction consistent with the rules but inconsistent with the spirit behind them." In other words, crooks will be crooked.

Baruch College Professor Abraham Briloff, noted for his assaults on rigged accounting, puts the whole thing in witty perspective. If the accountants hide behind the rules, suggests he, the public may come to view generally accepted accounting principles—GAAP—"as cleverly rigged accounting ploys". . . —CRAP. ■

August 1, 1975

2

THE
ACCOUNTING
ARENA

Accounting theory can sometimes get a bit tedious and *very* abstract. It's often easy to lose sight of the fact that accounting is an activity that not only reflects the real world but also affects the daily material lives of us all. Issues as diverse as the availability of gasoline and the cost of an American tourist's coffee in Cologne are influenced by the rules accountants write and the decisions they make. Accounting is chock-a-block with unbelievably difficult problems with a cast of colorful characters busily trying to solve them.

The seven following articles discuss various aspects of what you might call the Accounting Arena. We mean "arena" broadly: In part these seven pieces look at things accountants *do*—from justifying multimillion-dollar investments in money-losing professional sports franchises (see page 9) to arguing in stuffy European conference rooms about the virtues of *Ruckstellungen* (that's German for "reserves"; see page 38). Then too, these pieces introduce you to some of the seemingly intractible, sometimes just plain *weird*, hassles that accountants get into these days. For example: Should CPAs have access to information passed between lawyers and their corporate management clients? But what about the lawyer-client privileges? On the other hand, should lawyers be allowed to sue CPAs for failing to uncover a financial fraud (or simple mess) that might have been exposed if CPAs had had access to lawyer-client communications?

Hence the Accounting Arena, where, among others, you'll meet:

Noochie, the ex-CPA who couldn't keep his hands out of the till but who understands human nature better than most psychologists;

Portly Izaak Walton Bader, whose name chills Big Eight accounting firm partners with fright;

A Philadelphia finance director who presumably likes Philadelphia, dogs, and little children—but despises accountants who want to tell him how to keep his city's books.

Maybe you'll enjoy these individuals and their problems, find them funny. Perhaps not. But you'll no doubt agree that the Accounting Arena is in no way comprised of Elbert Hubbard's "boring little men with hearts of feldspar. . . who happily never reproduce and finally all go to hell."

Vince Lombardi:
Winning isn't everything,
it's the only thing.
Sports accountants:
Don't knock losing.

So there we were, brooding in a dark corner about where all the investors had gone, when Noochie, the ex-CPA, breezes in and sits at the bar. He's reading this newspaper clipping very intently. We look over his shoulder at the headline, "World Football League."

Noochie had a very good job once as a vice president of one of the Wall Street houses. Noochie also had a little thing going with the books about the time the senior partners decided on an independent audit. So Noochie is now doing people's income tax returns out of his apartment.

"What's a World Football League?" we ask Noochie. "Those beer bellies over in New Jersey that get knocked silly for $50 a game?"

Noochie sneers: "Boy are you dumb."

Noochie goes on, "Gary Davidson was through town yesterday"—and we understand. Gary Davidson is 39 years old and from California. He was an original promoter of the American Basketball Association in 1967, and last year he started the World Hockey Association. We laugh.

"What's he think he's doing? Howard Cosell would never let him start another league." But Noochie was indignant.

"I suppose you don't know that Frank Sinatra's in this and Spiro Agnew was going to be commissioner of the league until he got in trouble?" It's dreaming like this that gets Noochie in trouble.

"Come on. Who would invest in one of those things anyway? Unless you're the Knicks or the Celts or the Dolphins, you don't make any money off the gate or television either."

"That's *why* you go into it," he snorts. "Sports franchises are a tax

9

shelter. They generate nice tax losses because you can depreciate maybe 80 percent of the cost of the team by amortizing the cost of the player contracts. And you can pass through the losses to your main business, and when you sell, the profit is capital gains."

You don't argue with Noochie on matters like this, so we asked: "You amortize buildings and machinery. You don't amortize ballplayers, do you?" Noochie was patient.

"When you buy a team, the Internal Revenue Service lets you attribute a big part of the price to the value of the contracts with the players. To this you can apply straight-line depreciation. Which means you get a big chunk of your money back in three to five years in tax benefits.

"It works out real nice. Even if you sell the team for less than you paid, you still make a profit."

We looked lost. Noochie went on: "Yeah well, why else did CBS buy the [New York] Yankees from Dan Topping for $13.2 million and then sell them for $10 million?"

"Maybe it was a bad deal," we ventured. Noochie's nasty snicker drove us to call Gary Davidson. We asked what made him think people would be willing to risk money in yet another sports venture at a time when blue chips were going for peanuts.

Davidson speaks more elegantly than Noochie does. But he said the same thing: "Capital appreciation is the big factor. You buy a franchise in anticipation of the team's future market value."

As proof, Davidson points out that the first eight World Hockey Association teams cost their owners $25,800 each when the league was formed two years ago. The expansion teams this summer sold for $2 million per franchise, and the Winnipeg Jets recently turned down a $4.3-million offer to sell.

Wonderful for Winnipeg. But how many of those teams are making money? we asked. None of them yet, Davidson said. Moreover, insiders say that most of the teams in Davidson's other creation, the ABA, are still in the red after six years of operation. Yet the ABA and the WHA franchises *are* rising in value about as fast as the National Football League and the more profitable baseball major leagues.

It works, it turns out, something like this: The more you pay for the team, the higher value you can assign to the players and the more you can amortize. The more you amortize, the more you "lose." The more you lose, the more you reduce your outside income tax liabilities. So, who quibbles too much about price?

This might explain why some Washington, D.C. merchants are fighting with Seattle *and* a group of California investors, including composer Burt Bacharach, for the faltering San Diego Padres of C. Arnholt Smith's crumbling empire. It would also explain the saga of the Anaheim Amigos, an ABA charter team that cost the original owners $1.7 million out of pocket before they sold. Now the Amigos have become the Utah Stars out of Salt Lake City. The Stars won the 1971 ABA championship and were division leaders last year. The Stars have not yet made it into the black yet, but the franchise has been appraised recently at more than $5 million.

Next, we called Leslie Klinger, a Los Angeles tax lawyer whose firm represents sports teams.

"The owner of a sports team, whether he buys a new one or an established one, has roughly three kinds of assets. There's the sports and office equipment, but it doesn't amount to much. Then there is the franchise from the league, but the IRS has ruled that you cannot amortize it," Klinger told us.

"Finally, there are the contracts with the team members. A typical contract employs the player for one year and grants the team an option to renew the contract for a specified percentage of the player's previous salary. This is the so-called 'reserve' or option clause," he added. "The salary is renegotiated each year based on the player's performance last season. If there's no agreement, the player is bound by the option and cannot contract with another team. As a result, it is rare for a player to change teams through his own negotiations.

"The point is, the IRS says salaries must be expensed, but the *costs* of the contract—the   bonuses paid on signing or the extra cash paid another team for a player's contract—may be depreciated at a faster rate than they are paid, usually three to five years."

Then we came to the real goodies. Klinger continued: "And there's more. Because the option clause gives the owners such a tight hold over the players, the team itself has a 'future earnings' value that also is amortized. What the owner does then is go to the IRS with his team, for which he paid, say, $5 million, and try to get a depreciation ruling on the value of his players. He asks for as much as he can—usually 80 percent or 90 percent and the IRS whittles him down to 75 percent."

Of course, teams often don't generate operating earnings to offset these write-offs. But so what? "Most teams," says Klinger, "are limited partnerships or sole proprietorships, so you can pass through those losses."

"But remember," Klinger adds, " when the owner sells, even though the profit is a capital gain, all that depreciation he has taken is treated by the IRS as ordinary income."

When we reported this conversation to Noochie, he shot back: "So what? The owner had the money tax- and interest-free for those years."

Next, we called Mike Burke, president of Madison Square Garden, Inc., which owns both the Garden and the NBA Knicks. Burke had been an executive with the Yankees during the CBS years. The Yankees' trouble, he said, is that they were the *Yankees*, and the IRS assigned more value to the nondepreciable franchise and less to the depreciable contracts.

"We tried to write off $8.6 million (of the $13.2-million purchase price) *over six years*," Burke told us. "The IRS changed that to $6.5 million, I think." So it wasn't that good a deal. We hastened to confront Noochie.

"One bad deal doesn't explain why people are lined up to buy these franchises," he said airily. "I'll bet if you were on the inside you'd find most of these teams generate a lot of cash as well as extra tax losses for the owner's construction company or something. But you won't see the books because nearly all these deals are private."

And he was right about that. But one thing accomplished by the abortive attempt to merge the ABA with the senior basketball circuit, the NBA, was to set off a Congressional hearing on the matter.

One of those people who participated in the 1971 Congressional examination of big-time basketball was Benjamin A. Okner, an economist at the Brookings Institution. Okner is currently expanding a study he helped prepare for those hearings into a book on the economics of sports franchises.

"These guys are crying their way to the bank. We've made some projections on rates of return, and because of the straight-line depreciation feature, regardless of sport, the return on capital can be easily in the 10 percent to 15 percent range," Okner told us.

Okner produced some calculations based on an arbitrary team purchase price of $2 million. Okner's hypothetical team runs an operating profit of $100,000 before depreciation of the team contracts, whose amortization is a modest $300,000. So Okner's team is now running a $200,000 loss.

"Now the owner is presumably wealthy, say in the 70 percent bracket. So his personal tax liability is $140,000 out.

"But he also can take the real cash flow profits of $100,000 and put it in his pocket. That gives him a $240,000 return for the year, and that's 12 percent net of taxes," he added.

"And don't forget that many owners pay themselves or family members healthy salaries under the heading of 'general and administrative' costs."

Okner gave us something else to think about. The courts and Congress have really only established the reserve clause and the de facto monopoly status of the four pro team sports in the last five years or so. It is from those rulings that the big depreciation allowances flow. What Okner suggests is that many of the new team owners are likely to sell their franchises every five years or so—once they are written down. Why? The trend toward bonus-fat pools of player contracts makes the new teams more salable than older franchises, where the write-offs may not be as big nor the owners as willing to move.

"Watch baseball and some of the original American Football League owners in the next year or so. I think you will see a lot of franchise swapping and sales across the country. The newer hockey and basketball teams shouldn't be far behind," Okner predicted. "That way they can pick up new partners and start depreciating the same players all over again."

Noochie sneered at that: "What do you expect from a bunch of foundation guys? Foundations don't pay taxes, they're against tax shelters."

Noochie may not be the straightest guy in the world. But he sure knows human nature. ■

December 15, 1973

B "Everybody picks on us"

I. (for Izaak) Walton Bader is a portly man in his mid-50s. We found him bustling about the cramped, faded, paper-strewn offices of Bader & Bader in midtown Manhattan with great enterprise and surprising agility. To all appearances, he seemed just another hardworking lawyer whose practice was not especially prosperous.

Ah, but appearances can be deceiving. Walton Bader is the scourge of the U.S. accounting profession. A man whose name strikes fear in the hearts of senior partners in the big certified public accounting firms.

He is one of perhaps a dozen trial lawyers who specialize in stockholder class-action suits against accounting firms. As recently as 1962 there were perhaps two lawsuits pending against major CPA firms; today there are over 200. And if the smaller accounting firms were included, the estimated number of pending legal suits is at least 500.

Scarcely a day seems to go by but that some accounting firm agrees to settle out of court on one of these class actions (Arthur Young's $950,000 settlement on the Commonwealth United case). Or is being disciplined with unusual severity by the Securities & Exchange Commision (Touche Ross's recent consent to "peer review" by outside CPAs because of alleged "improper conduct" on its 1970 and 1971 audits of U.S. Financial). Or is itself threatening to sue the SEC (Arthur Andersen, following the recent acquittal of Andersen staffers in a criminal fraud suit involving Four Seasons Nursing Homes).

Not surprisingly, the accounting profession is feeling persecuted, beset on all sides by hecklers and enemies.

How justified is all this litigation? When we got down to cases, we soon discovered that plaintiffs' lawyers like Walton Bader sometimes ask good ques- tions—questions the accounting profession ought to have been asking itself long before. Bader: "If you have a company that says it has $1 million of inventory in stock, and I'm your auditor, am I supposed to take your word for it or take a spot check?"

Hypothetical? Not at all. Bader was talking about Equity Funding. Haskins & Sells (and later, Seidman & Seidman) were the auditors for Equity Funding's life insurance subsidiary. The "inventory" of a life insurance com- pany is, of course, its policies. But the auditors allegedly never did a spot check to see that the inventory was there—that is, to see that policyholders had actually received their policies.

Naturally, the two firms won't discuss a case that's in litigation, so we asked Victor Earle III, house counsel for Peat Marwick Mitchell & Co., to com- ment. He saw nothing much wrong with the way Equity Funding's life insur- ance subsidiary had been audited. Earle: "It's my understanding that H&S did *not* confirm policies with policyholders because that's not what's done in in- surance accounting."

Not what you do? In other words, the accountants normally just take management's word for it that those life insurance policies exist in the hands of policyholders?

"Well," Earle continued, "I know the American Institute of Certified Public Accountants has appointed a committee to consider whether the pro- fession *should* confirm with policyholders. Of course, you can always defraud auditors if you're really clever about it."

Back to Bader: "If they don't take a spot check, and they're wrong in their certification, then they've got to take the responsibility, that's all."

Bader was far from finished. Outright fraud was quite rare, he said. More typical were cases of misleading financial statements. How about an example, we asked.

"Cartridge Television!" he shot back. "Here's a company that has filed for bankruptcy. The majority holder, Avco, has offered creditors 10 cents on the dollar!"

Exactly what bothered him about that 1971 prospectus he was waving about?

"O.K.," Bader replied, turning to the financial statements. "Look here. They show assets of $8,401,783 and liabilities of $6,434,681, so that means there's a net worth of about $2 million in the company, right? But they have a little note here that says research and preoperating costs, since we haven't had any sales, are being *deferred*. Now there are $6 million of research and preoperating costs being deferred, and therefore they don't show up on the lia- bility side of the balance sheet. Now if they *did*, you'd have a company with a $4-million net deficit, right?"

But, we asked, wasn't Arthur Young, the auditors of Cartridge Television only following generally accepted accounting principles?

"Listen, companies do this to jazz up stock prices," said Bader with exasperation. "You can call those R&D costs a current expense, or you can say this thing will have a useful life of five years, and therefore I will depreciate it over that life, but you don't just go defer that expense *completely*. You're giving unsophisticated investors the impression that the company is making money."

But if Cartridge Television had expensed that $6 million in R&D costs, we said, they would have shown a sizable loss. How could they have raised any public money?

"You just explain that the loss results from the expensing of these research & development expenses," Bader replied. "People understand this."

A trivial, nit-picking complaint? Evidently, the Financial Accounting Standards Board doesn't think so. On Mar. 15 it held public hearings on the topic of how to account for research and development expenses, with particular emphasis on how those expenses should be handled in developing companies like Cartridge Television.

Why They Settle

Thus do lawyers like Walton Bader justify their suits against the accounting profession. But what do the targets, the accountants, have to say? After all, most of the major CPA firms carry insurance against such things.

Yes, but had we considered the *size* of the damages sought in some of these actions, the accountants shot back. Take Equity Funding, for example. Somewhere around 65 separate class actions had been filed on that one. (As it happens, Walton Bader is counsel for what he says is the largest group of shareholders in any of these actions.) Just *one* of those actions, filed against the auditors for Equity Funding's life insurance subsidiary, seeks over $500 million in damages.

At those kind of stakes, you settle out of court rather than risk a "guilty" jury verdict.

"I can't think of a single class-action suit against accountants that's ever been litigated," answered one senior partner of a major CPA firm. Much too risky, explained Peat Marwick's Earle: "I watched the jurors in the criminal action against Coopers & Lybrand partners in the Continental Vending case. They were looking out the window! When a guy's life and career are on the line and the jurors are looking out the window, it gets a little nerve-wracking! So you worry about the jury and you worry even more about the uncertainty of the law in this area.'"

The result, he went on, is that out-of-court settlements by CPA firms have been growing bigger and more frequent. There have been at least a dozen major settlements of over $1 million in the past several years. And what started it all was the $5-million settlement by Coopers & Lybrand in 1970 in the Mill Factors case. "That just attracts the plaintiffs' lawyers like flies!" said Earle.

Not surprisingly, the accountants take a very dim view of the "plaintiffs' lawyers" who bring such actions against them. Ralph Kent, a senior partner of Arthur Young: "There is a limited element of the bar that makes the old-time ambulance chasers in the legal profession look like choirboys. We're going to have to develop some way of getting at that element for malicious prosecution."

Lately, however, even "nice" lawyers have been getting into the act, according to Victor Earle: "There have been some lawsuits against accounting firms—even our own—where very responsible law firms have been involved. This is one of the trends I find rather ominous. A bank that invested in, say, Penn Central [a Peat Marwick client] may think: 'We lost all this money, and our shareholders must be wondering why we aren't taking some action.' So they sue everybody in sight."

Still, it is hard to shed many tears for the accountants. Even some top accountants we talked to felt that CPA firms may be making large settlements not simply to avoid litigation but because they have something to hide. Said one senior partner of a Big Eight CPA firm: "You almost have to judge these settlements in terms of the amount of money involved. If you settle for, say, $200,000, that might indicate that you just want to stop the legal expense. But if you settle for $2 million or $3 million, that might suggest that maybe there is something involved that you don't want to expose. Even a settlement approaching $1 million gets on the high side to me."

This reminded us of a recent SEC action against Whitaker Corp. Last year, Arthur Andersen reportedly settled for $875,000 when client Whittaker Corp. threatened to sue because an Arthur Andersen audit had failed to uncover a $6.3-million inventory shortfall in a subsidiary. Several weeks ago, however, the SEC took Whittaker to court charging that it had failed to disclose that Arthur Andersen had also done nearly $1.4 million worth of *free* consulting work for the company. This suggests that the true size of Arthur Andersen's settlement with Whittaker was over $2 million.

If the lawyers weren't problem enough, the SEC, too, keeps getting tougher with the accountants. Several weeks ago the SEC certainly put the bite on Touche Ross & Co. for its auditing work at troubled U.S. Financial. In addition to public rebukes by SEC Chief Accountant John C. (Sandy) Burton (who was quoted as saying, "There were grounds for the greatest skepticism, and Touche Ross didn't exercise it."), the Commission ordered: 1) that Touche Ross not undertake any work for an SEC-registered real estate company for one year, 2) that its San Diego office not accept any new SEC business for one year, 3) that it submit to the Commission its procedures for detecting management involvement in significant corporate transactions, and 4) that next year its work be reviewed by auditors outside the firm — the "peer review" scheme devised by Sandy Burton and applied only once before.

The accountants were as furious with the SEC as they are with private lawyers. "I don't really think the SEC is qualified to initiate peer review," said Ralph Kent of Arthur Young. "Accounting firms have a competence in auditing that is a high multiple of the depth of that competence that exists in the SEC." In a client letter dated February 1974, Chairman Harvey Kapnick of Arthur Andersen & Co. angrily threatened to sue the SEC as a result of a recent criminal trial of Andersen staffers involved in Four Seasons Nursing Homes. There had been, wrote Kapnick, "significant improprieties by government representatives in this case from beginning to end" and "a reckless disregard of the facts as well as personal liberties."

Peat Marwick's Earle warned that such persecution would cause the profession to avoid taking hard-nosed stands: "Take Republic Life Insurance. They put out a press release we thought was wrong about an increased loan-loss reserve. We forced them to put out a new press release the next day saying the increased loan-loss reserve would reflect on prior years. Our reward? We got hit with a $25-million class action the next day."

But Earle is begging the question a bit. In 1972 the SEC complained when, under very similar circumstances in a National Student Marketing prospectus, Peat Marwick said nothing. And in the Republic Life case, the SEC now charges that the real question is not whether the original press release made earlier financial statements not comparable, but whether Republic was conspiring to hide its failing investment in Realty Equities.

So, it is hard to have too much sympathy for the accountants. As lawyer Walton Bader puts it: "You involve them in damage claims in the millions of dollars, and pretty soon it reminds the accountants of their responsibilities to the investing public." Quite obviously, before Sandy Burton of the SEC got after them and until the lawsuits got rolling, the accountants needed some reminding. "Professional standards" alone didn't do the trick.

As SEC Commissioner A.A. Sommer Jr. put it last fall: ". . .the accounting profession has matured with the result that more is expected of it and it is presumably able to reach levels of responsibility. . .financial, legal, and ethical."

Amen. ∎

April 1, 1974

EPILOGUE: In April 1978, I. Walton Bader and other lawyers and their clients interested in suing accounting firms won a major legal round: The U.S. Court of Appeals for the Second Circuit (New York) ruled that securities brokerage firm customers do have the right to sue accounting firms for damages if the accounting firms have prepared false and misleading audits of the brokerage house.

The case at hand involved Big Eight public accounting firm

Touche Ross & Co., whose securities brokerage house client Weis Securities Inc. collapsed in 1973. (Five Weis Securities officers were later sentenced to prison terms for fraud.) The defunct firm's trustee and the Securities Investors Protection Corp. (SIPC) alleged that Touche Ross certified 1972 Weis Securities financial statements that later proved to be false and misleading. The trustee and SIPC sued Touche Ross for a total of $65 million. Touche Ross denied the plaintiff's allegations—and claimed that Weis customers had no right, under the 1934 Securities and Exchange Acts, to sue a brokerage house's auditors in the first place. The court disagreed with Touche Ross on their contention that Weis customers had no recourse to the auditors. Wrote Judge Edward Lumbard:

> Certified public accountants play a significant role in the scheme created by the 1934 Act for the regulation of securities trading. . . .Both [the SEC] and SIPC as well as brokers' customers must rely on the certification by accountants. . .Accordingly, we rule that a private remedy is an essential supplement to the scheme of enforcement. . .

Touche Ross announced it would probably appeal the judgement to the Supreme Court and stressed again the firm is not culpable.

Said Touche Ross general counsel Richard Murray to a *Wall Street Journal* reporter: "Two parties that were in the best position to criticize our service—the SEC and the U.S. Attorney's office—concluded that we, too, were victimized by a massive fraud by Weis management. The only people who are suing us are parties looking for a deep pocket to share losses."

Assuming it stands, Judge Lumbard's decision narrows significantly the deep-pockets' maneuvering room. And this is a real and increasingly distressing problem for CPAs.

In mid-1977, not long after courts assessed some $39 million in damages against four CPA firms involved in the giant Equity Funding Corp. scandal, a CPA firm partner fretted to a FORBES reporter: "It's horrifying. One partner in one office makes one slip at anytime, and my entire life's work could vanish!"

Two things that *won't* vanish are the deepening flap between the CPAs and the public they are supposed to serve—and the flap between the CPAs and the lawyers, another side of which battle is exposed in the following selection.

The lawyers
vs.
the accountants

Westinghouse Electric is in trouble over its long-term contracts to supply uranium to its electrical utility customers. In theory, the loss could run as high as $2.5 billion, wiping out WX's equity capital. Top executives have probably known of the exposure for some time. But they notified their customers only in September of this year and have yet to disclose it officially to their stockholders. Should it have been disclosed earlier to all concerned?

In 1971 the State of California sued Boise Cascade for misrepresentation in the sale of recreation land in California. Class-action suits followed, and Boise ended up shelling out $60 million. The potential liability was not disclosed to stockholders until the suit was filed in October 1971. Yet Boise Cascade executives must have known that they were getting complaining letters from unhappy land buyers and that the state had sued others for the same kinds of sales practices.

Both cases have a common feature. There existed a *potential* liability well in advance of the *actual* liability. Management knew the potential liability was serious. But still, it did not tell stockholders about the sword hanging overhead.

These are what are known as "unasserted claims." In such a case, the potential plaintiff may not even know he has a case; but management does.

Right now "unasserted claims" are the subject of a battle royal between lawyers and accountants. The accountants are increasingly anxious to avoid being sued by stockholders. They want to cross every "t" and dot every "i." To help avoid surprises, they want their clients' outside law firms to tell them what they know about potential claims as well as actual claims. The accountants already require such information from house counsel as well as from top management. Now they want another assurance, this time from the supposedly more independent outside counsel. Has management asked advice about some potential lawsuit that might have a material impact? If so, the accountants want to know—even if management feels it is not serious.

Corporate lawyers are horrified. They feel they are being asked, in effect, to spy on their clients for the protection of the accountants. Not the least of the damage this would do would be to advertise potential claims to potential plaintiffs.

"It's a real tough one," says John Burton, chief accountant at the Securities & Exchange Commission. "If you disclose it, then the contingency occurs. If you don't disclose it, and the contingency occurs anyway, then you've got one big peck of trouble because then you've failed to disclose a material contingency."

The principles involved are not new. In the late Fifties the accountants got together and defined what they regarded as "contingent liabilities." They included "unasserted claims" in the definition. The lawyers, however, did *not* regard "unasserted claims" as actual liabilities.

The disagreement remained largely academic until the Seventies. Suddenly the accountants found themselves being sued on all sides. They began looking for every possible way to protect themselves. Soon they demanded that the lawyers tell them about potential claims and liabilities. The lawyers, citing client confidentiality, refused.

Unfortunately, there are no easy answers. When, after all, did the Boise Cascade situation cease being just an annoyance and start being a multimillion-dollar liability? Or when did the price of uranium reach the crisis stage for Westinghouse?

The whole situation is a terrible can of worms. With the ever-growing tangle of federal, state and local laws, it is a rare company that operates wholly within the law at all times. Patent infringement, inadvertent encroachment on another company's property, discrimination against women, illegal campaign gifts, perhaps even foreign bribes, are all examples of unasserted claims.

The auditors feel that if the assertion of such a claim seems "probable" and the consequences may be adverse and material, the existence of the unasserted claim should be disclosed in the interests of fair financial disclosure. Thus, Telex' auditors forced it to disclose in 1973 that it might be liable for claims due to misleading fourth-quarter statements.

The problem gets stickier. To whom does management owe its allegiance? To the general public? Or to its present stockholders? Had Westinghouse revealed its uranium problem earlier, it might have warned off some potential buyers of its stock—which dropped 40 percent after the disclosure. But early disclosure might have hurt existing stockholders. "Nobody seems to consider the current shareholders," complains attorney Abraham M. Stanger, a member of the joint lawyer-auditor committee that has been meeting for two years to try to resolve the issue.

What pits the lawyers against the accountants is that auditors don't always have ways of knowing about these unasserted claims; they don't, after all, appear on the books. First, the auditors must ask management whether such claims exist. Second, to verify from independent sources what management tells them, they turn to the company's lawyers. The idea is that if the boss is lying, professional ethics will force the lawyers to contradict him. If both lie to the accountant, the accountant can claim that, like the shareholders, he, too, was deceived; presumably he's off the hook.

In short, the lawyers are being asked to pull the accountants' chestnuts out of the fire.

If unasserted claims are a headache for the accountants, they are poison for lawyers. There is no problem for the lawyers if top management agrees that the company faces a potential claim; then all the lawyers have to do is advise auditors of the existence of the potential claim and their opinion of its likely consequences. But suppose management insists there is no claim, but the lawyers believe there is? What then? Does the lawyer squeal to the auditors? That could violate the sanctity of client-counsel relations.

Listen to the horrified reaction of a prominent attorney, Joseph Hinsey, a partner in the New York firm of White & Case: "We should not be pressured into making third-party disclosures in such a way as to emasculate our ability to function as legal advisers." And Hinsey isn't just speaking for himself. He is chairman of the American Bar Association's Committee on Audit Inquiry Responses—in short, he's the man on this particular firing line.

Hinsey raises this point: If management could not depend on the confidentiality of what it tells its lawyers, it might be reluctant to discuss important matters with them; the entire relationship would be upset.

Hinsey points out that the lawyers are not trying to avoid their audit responsibilities. If a lawyer feels that his advice has been ignored and that non-disclosure would be a violation of the criminal or securities law, he would be obligated to resign under the ABA's Code of Professional Responsibility. Hinsey argues that, in the absence of a resignation, the auditors should assume that there is no such violation or at least that there is none of which the lawyers are aware. That looks like a clear signal to the accountants. But it isn't.

The trouble is that Hinsey is only talking about situations where a claim is "probable" and likely to be adverse and material. But probability is so tightly defined by the lawyers that there would have to be a 95 percent chance of a claim. Very few cases are that certain. As it now stands, without that near certainty, the lawyers will talk to the auditors only about unasserted claims that management itself is willing to disclose. The lawyers say their responsibility goes no further.

The lawyers have a real problem. It was dramatized in Tulsa last month when a federal judge threw Arthur Young partner William Grant in jail for contempt. Grant had refused to turn over to a federal grand jury two documents—one of which was a lawyers' letter—involved in an audit of Phillips Petroleum. Phillips is under federal grand jury investigation for possible tax fraud arising from $495,000 in illegal campaign gifts over a nine-year period.

The grand jury couldn't have gotten the lawyers' letter from the attorneys; it would have been covered by the client privilege. But the grand jury did get it from the jailed accountant after one night behind bars.

The fact is that while lawyers' relations with their clients are protected by confidentiality, an auditor's relationship is not. What the lawyer tells the auditor today, the world may know tomorrow—not because auditors are chatterboxes, but because their work papers, unlike those of lawyers, are subject to subpoena.

A Dreaded Phrase

The auditors are not weaponless in this battle. If the lawyers keep mum, the auditors can whisper "scope qualification." That's a tough phrase. A "scope qualification" informs stockholders that the examination was limited and that, therefore, the auditor is not entirely sure that it is fair. That does it. The SEC will not accept a scope-qualified annual report. Presto! The corporation is in hot water. No annual meeting. No stock trading.

So the argument rages, and the politeness is beginning to wear thin. The accountants threaten scope qualification. The lawyers talk about the lawyer-client relationship. Both sides have hardened their stands. In late October, the American Institute Of Certified Public Accountants issued a proposed statement that would *require* auditors to scope-qualify a report where they received what they regarded as an unsatisfactory response from lawyers. This came on the heels of a proposed statement from the ABA that would require lawyers to refuse to respond to auditors on unasserted claims except with specific authorization of management.

You can't blame the accountants for not wanting to be sued. But White & Case's Joe Hinsey asks: Why us? Why the lawyers? He argues: "The auditors are not being told to make inquiry of corporate economists about the possibility of losses from currency devaluation. They don't ask lobbyists about the chances of reductions in the oil depletion allowance. An unasserted claim is just one of a host of general business contingencies that may visit loss upon a company."

The accountants' answer is that devaluation and changes in the law are *future* events, whereas unasserted claims refer to events that have already taken place.

Who is right? Fortunately— or unfortunately—both sides are right. A compromise is called for. Right now, the ABA-AICPA committee is meeting to find ways out of the impasse. The ABA could loosen the definition of probability and require the lawyer to resign if management overrules his advice to disclose unasserted claims. Or it could allow indirect communication with the auditors.

That way, the lawyer wouldn't have to tattle on his employer; but neither would he be acquiescing in sweeping something under the rug. There wouldn't be many occasions for resignation, but the threat would be there and the accountants would feel a bit less vulnerable.

But please, fellows, settle the argument with a minimum of paperwork and additional cost to the businessman, who is already groaning under the burden of auditing and legal costs. It's like a lot of things in the world today: In our anxiety to protect one set of rights absolutely, we sometimes damage another set of rights. And get ever more entangled in red tape. ■

December 1, 1975

Forecasting earnings

Should they be forecast? Or shouldn't they?

One reason the public feels it is getting a raw deal in the stock market is that it never knows about earnings declines or increases until it reads about them in the newspaper. By then the damage is done—or the goodies are gone. If Wall Street and its institutional customers can get a pretty good idea about earnings in <u>advance</u>, why shouldn't the general public? That's what Securities & Exchange Commission Chairman William J. Casey wants to know. He proposes: Let management make their internal forecasts public and let everybody have equal access to them. The forecast may be right or it may be wrong, but at least everybody gets it at the same time.

Is forecasting a good idea?

Corporation executives, brokerage houses and certified public accountants are divided. To get the pro and the con, FORBES *interviewed two certified public accountants. The men and their views:*

Pro

Donald H. Chapin of Arthur Young & Co. is chairman of the subcommittee on forecasting the accounting procedures of the American Institute of Certified Public Accountants. He says flatly: "I predict that the SEC will soon require that forecasts be included in prospectuses." And he welcomes the idea. Chapin made a study of the British system for the AICPA and he says it works—for the

Con

Harvey Kapnick is chairman and chief executive of Arthur Andersen & Co. He says: "The first question is whether forecasts should be published at all. All of us familiar with forecasting know that forecasts are not reliable. Conditions are constantly changing. How can you keep people informed of the changes?"

Kapnick insists a CPA has done his job when he certifies a financial

25

Pro

benefits of management and investors alike.

Chapin expects the SEC to adopt something like the British system, which does not require certified forecasts in prospectuses for new issues except in the case of mergers and acquisitions. However, he would not object to a regulation requiring certified forecasts for new issues. He says: "All the chartered accountants I talked with in London said they were willing to report on new issues.

Chapin says the British system helps the investors because "the charted accountants [as CPAs in the U.K. are called] lend substantial reliability to management forecasts." He says, "It makes the forecasts better. Managements frequently look at the future through rose-colored glasses. They have no objectivity about themselves and what they're doing. In the U.K. the chartered accountants have brought them down to earth."

He admits that requiring CPAs to approve forecasts will create certain difficulties. "There is no doubt that when forecasts first appear they will be accorded greater validity than they deserve by some unsophisticated investors," he says. "Some managements will put too much conservatism in their numbers in an attempt to protect themselves, and a few may use forecasts to manipulate the market."

Quite aside from that, he adds, "forecasts, by their very nature, can go wrong in five minutes."

Con

statement. That is a record of the past. Predictions of the future, based on this record, "must be the responsibility of the investor. This is the essence of risk-taking, and predicting and interpreting the future is the primary function in investment valuation. Risk-taking is at the heart of the free enterprise system, and the investor may either reap rewards or incur losses. No one can undertake to insure the results of future events."

For the investor, Kapnick sees two great dangers in certified forecasts. One is that management will be overly conservative in estimating sales and earnings in order not to get egg on its face when the results come in. This might dissuade investors from putting money into a company with a much brighter future than its management is willing to attest to publicly. The other is that some managements will overestimate future sales and earnings in order to boost the stock. "There could be scandals," says Kapnick.

In addition, Kapnick fears that requiring certified forecasts would create "a conflict of interest in the accounting profession." Would not a CPA be tempted, he asks, to make annual reports bear out the predictions he attested to?

"There have been suggestions that one firm should certify the forecasts and another the annual reports," Kapnick notes. "That would just double the costs," he says.

Kapnick doubts that CPAs are really qualified to certify fore-

Pro

Chapin admits to other possible difficulties. "I believe forecasts should be published only in those circumstances where a reasonable degree of reliability can be expected, and, unfortunately, the SEC does not seem to be as impressed as they should be with this problem." An even greater problem, he says, is Section 11 of the Securities Act of 1933. Under one interpretation of this act, a certified public accountant might be open to suit if a prospectus he approved contained any misleading statements or failed to include any relevant facts. Chapin feels the SEC should clarify Section 11 as regards the CPAs.

"All of these factors notwithstanding," says Chapin, "I think that the SEC will come to the conclusion that our profession should be put to work to increase the reliability of published forecasts, because the CPA's objectivity and accounting and auditing skills can be effective in increasing the reliability of some types of forecasts." ∎

Con

casts. And he questions whether they have a right to. "All forecasts are based on assumptions," he points out, "a 17 percent rise in sales, an 18 percent rise, 19 percent, 20 percent. Does a CPA have any right to make a management change its assumptions? Does a CPA have the right to say, 'You can't hope for more than 16 percent? He wasn't hired to run the company."

Yes, says Kapnick, it would be good for his business—and the accounting profession generally—if the SEC required ceritifed forecasts. "It would greatly enlarge our revenues." However, Kapnick also believes it would involve the profession in a welter of litigation. In the U.K., he points out, there's no provision for class actions, and solicitors are forbidden to take cases on a contingency basis. That keeps the number of suits against chartered accountants down to cases where there is reason to assume the accountants consciously misled investors. Here, there's no such restraint. ∎

December 1, 1972

EPILOGUE: Although the SEC had not, when this book was published, *required* corporate managements to forecast earnings, the Commission was certainly *encouraging* forecasts. And the FASB seemed headed in the same direction. In November 1978 the FASB published Statement of Financial Accounting Concepts No. 1: "Objectives of Financial Reporting by Business Enterprises." This Statement says, among other things, that financial reporting should be *future*-oriented. Said former SEC chief accountant and longtime earnings forecast advocate John C. (Sandy) Burton to a *New York Times* reporter when the statement was released: "It (the Statement) doesn't say management has to publish forecasts, but it does mean that financial statements which report what happened last year can't ignore mentioning dramatic developments since. It remains to be seen if management will be legally held responsible if it ignores this, but the effect will surely heighten management's responsibility and to make financial statements do what they were meant to do."

How do you keep city hall honest?

It's self-serving of accountants to want to audit municipal books. But there is good reason to think that it's about time.

"This is all a lot of gunk and hogwash!" says Lennox Moak. "Just another part of the poker game. More people who want to tell us how to run our business and collect a fee for it."

Moak is entitled to vent a little steam. As Director of Finances for deficit-ridden Philadelphia, he's used to people looking over his shoulder. He's also president of the 5,800-member Municipal Finance Officers Association. What he refers to as "gunk and hogwash" is the first in-depth report on financial disclosure policies of 46 major U.S. cities. It's a 44-page opus entitled, logically enough, *Financial Disclosure Practices of the American Cities*, just released jointly by the University of Michigan and one of the Big Eight CPA firms, Coopers & Lybrand.

Essentially the study supports proposed federal legislation that would require cities to keep their books as if they were publicly held corporations. Current voluntary municipal accounting guidelines are not fully complied with, the study says, and even if they were they wouldn't provide useful information about financial condition. Norman Auerbach, Coopers & Lybrand's new managing partner and the man who directed the study, calls it "an important first step toward restoring credibility" to city finances.

Not everyone agrees. "So who am I going to send my annual report to?" asks exasperated Los Angeles Treasurer Robert M. Odell. "Doesn't Coopers & Lybrand realize that 98 percent of Los Angeles' bonds are 'bearer bonds,' meaning that the city has no record of names and addresses for the people who hold those bonds?"

The answer to Odell's question, of course, is that *prospective* investors are the ones who need that annual report—as a means of restoring the credibility of urban paper.

29

Municipal finance men will have none of that, however. Their defense is the Constitution's doctrine of separate powers (*i.e.,* states' rights). So what if the Securities & Exchange Commission demanded Philadelphia's financial records last June? "I haven't given them a damned thing!" says Moak, who proceeded to take the SEC to court on the matter.

But help for the SEC has come from a strange quarter. Arthur Andersen, which is busy suing the SEC on other matters, has recently submitted to Congress opinions from two eminent law firms disputing the cities' claims on constitutional grounds.

The accounting "system" Moak and his compatriots are fighting to defend is referred to in the trade as GAAFR or, more formally, Governmental Accounting, Auditing and Financial Reporting.

Compared with GAAP (Generally Accepted Accounting Principles), say the accountants, GAAFR is . . . well, primitive.

To begin with, accountants explain, a government accounting system such as GAAFR is really a sugar bowl accounting technique. Rents are paid from one bowl, payrolls from another, typewriters and cars bought from a third and fourth. "GAAFR was designed with legal compliance in mind," says Auerbach of Coopers & Lybrand. "What you get from GAAFR is more of a detailed dollar accounting than a statement of financial condition. Now we don't say all GAAFR practices are bad—they're fine for internal reporting. But we do say they don't go to the heart of public reporting objectives—apprising the public of a city's financial condition."

Auerbach clearly has a point. If you want to invest in $36-billion (revenues) General Motors, for example, you can send for GM's 1975 annual report. Twenty-four tidy pages summarizing GM's 1975 financial condition. But if you want to invest in $527-million-revenues Detroit, the annual report you'll receive is about useless. It is over 150 pages long and is replete with thousands of numbers for hundreds of Detroit sugar bowl transactions, from a grant for an Indian exhibit to library book costs. It is as if GM sent you detailed information on the transactions of every single one of its divisions, subdivisions and sub-subdivisions.

Nor is Detroit's annual report extraordinary. Chicago's report runs to 448 pages, Boston's to 900. As Gilman C. Gunn III, senior municipal bond analyst for the Chubb Corp., recently told a Senate committee: "Individual investors . . . don't have the background to wade through a budget document the size of a Manhattan telephone book."

Some municipal finance officers reluctantly agree that consolidated reports would better serve the public. New York City Comptroller Harrison Goldin even included such a summary in last year's 568-page report—for the first time.

But the accountants say this isn't enough. They point out that the GAAFR accounting system is not full-accrual bookkeeping, with the result that investors cannot compare cities' reports with those issued by publicly held companies. More important, horrendous future liabilities can be (and have been) hidden away even if the GAAFR accounting system is fully complied with.

For example, GAAFR rules do not require cities to accrue unpaid sick leave and vacation time, except in footnote disclosure. "And we think cities that omit significant amounts of these liabilities are just kidding people about their true financial positions," says John Fox, who is a municipal accounting specialist at Coopers & Lybrand.

Or take fixed-asset accounting. Under GAAFR, cities need not calculate depreciation on many of their fixed assets—from the bureaucrat's free cars to their secretaries' typewriters. GAAFR merely requires accounting for assets acquired; it is not concerned with reporting the cost of using those assets. "And the cost of using a fixed asset is something that taxpayers should be aware of," says Fox. Needless to say, *no* city likes the idea of complying with the SEC's new replacement cost rules—even though they are as important for cities as for companies.

For reasons like these, the Coopers & Lybrand study urges cities to use the same accounting and reporting practices required of companies.

To this, the local financemen have no sound rejoinders. Some harp on GAAP's well-known deficiencies. "Penn Central used GAAP accounting," says one city's treasurer, "and how well were its investors protected?" True, but irrelevant. Philadelphia's Lennox Moak even claims that GAAFR can produce more conservative results than can GAAP. How so? "All my accounts receivable are 100 percent reserved. But under GAAP I'd have to report the difference between my accounts receivable and my reserves for uncollectible accounts as an asset. So I'd be forced to show a $60-million surplus."

Isn't that good?

"No! I'd be in the ludicrous position of showing a surplus when I'm trying to get new taxes. I could talk to the city council until hell freezes over, and still not be able to explain it to them."

In other words, GAAFR may not make good accounting sense, but it does make good pork-barrel sense. Even so the cities comply with GAAFR selectively—*very* selectively. According to the Coopers & Lybrand report, only about 24 percent of the surveyed cities disclose unfunded vested pension liabilities. Just 7 percent disclose non-capitalized lease obligations. Nearly half say nothing about their accounting procedures. Yet GAAFR says all these, and more, must be disclosed.

To this the local financemen reply rather lamely: The marketplace never demanded the information from us, so we never supplied it. A study to be released late this month by the Municipal Finance Officers Association (MFOA) will show that prospectus disclosure by cities has increased substantially since New York's crisis hit the headlines. Thus the cities' finance officers say voluntary compliance, goaded by market demand, makes federally mandated disclosure unnecessary, expensive and perhaps even counterproductive.

The politicians, reluctant to accept the kind of standards they enjoy forcing on businessmen, finally fall back on accusing the accounting firms of greed. Their contention is that the accounting firms are drooling at the prospect of 40,000 potential customers out there among the state and local governments.

"I think you can put the big accounting firms in two classes," says a business school professor working for the municipal finance officers group. "On the one hand are the Coopers & Lybrands and Arthur Andersens actively trying to get legislation passed to create demand for their services. On the other are firms like Peat Marwick Mitchell who feign disapproval of such laws in the hopes that when the laws do come, the cities will remember them as their friends."

Of course, the Coopers & Lybrand study does not call for CPA-audited municipal reports. Said a Coopers & Lybrand spokesman: "We certainly do feel they *should* be audited. But being a CPA firm, we thought it might seem self-serving if we came out and said it."

The underwriters are out for *their* interests, too. They fear investors will sue them for the cities' disclosure deficiencies. Hence the plea of Richard Kezer, Citibank senior vice president and Dealer Bank Association president, to a Senate committee early this year: "This is one reason we support prompt federal legislation to deal with municipal securities disclosure."

So far the cities have managed to stall progress on Senators John Tower (Rep., Tex.) and Harrison Williams' (Dem., N.J.) Municipal Securities Full Disclosure Act. An aide to Senator Tower says the bill will go nowhere this year, and probably nowhere in 1977. "I think it would take a new city crisis to get it passed," he says. As for Philadelphia's Moak, he says he will fight such legislation. "We will not delegate responsibility to the accounting fraternity to decide what we should do and then by law of Congress be forced to do what they tell us to. The accountants don't stand in the rain with us when the going gets tough."

But that's just the point. There is little question that the people who will be buying municipal debt in the future will demand audited financial statements sooner or later—so that the auditors *will* stand in the rain with the cities when the going gets tough as they are being forced to do with corporations.

Isn't that what public auditors are for? ■

October 1, 1976

EPILOGUE: Late in 1978 the City of Cleveland defaulted on some $15 million of its notes. The default triggered plans to sack thousands of city workers—and again raised the question: Why *shouldn't* state and local borrowers be required to keep their books the way corporate borrowers are made to keep (and have audited) their books?

The Financial Accounting Standards Board is moving gingerly, to be sure—towards setting standards for municipal accounting standard setting and auditing. In June 1978, the FASB issued a discussion memorandum, "Conceptual Framework for Financial Accounting and Reporting: Objectives of Financial Reporting by Nonbusiness Organizations" which in effect suggests first the Board can (and, we infer, will) set accounting rules for nonbusiness enterprises—meaning nonprofit organizations like foundations, museums . . . and state and local governments. The Municipal Finance Officers Association immediately ordered 300 copies of the FASB's memorandum and vowed once again to fight the FASB should the Board attempt to set municipal financial reporting standards.

We don't know where this will end. But it is clear that the battle lines are drawn. It will be a fight worth watching.

Realism?
Or fairy tales?

What is the proper goal of financial reporting? 1) To soothe stockholders, to make them happy? Or, 2) to present as accurate a picture as possible of the true situation?

If you think the answer is No. Two, you are not aware of the controversy over reserves for future losses. It seems that some insurance companies have begun setting aside a portion of their earnings against the day when a hurricane or flood hits them with huge losses. Only prudent, you say? But wait a minute. On closer examination, there is something seriously amiss here. That is why the Financial Accounting Standards Board is debating the issue.

Catastrophe reserves are a relatively new phenomenon. They have sprung up only in the past three years. Although the FASB has identified only a dozen insurance companies with these reserves, among them Hartford Fire, Firemen's Fund, Aetna, CNA and Travelers, they represent 20 percent of the total property and casualty premiums. These companies take a portion of current income each year and charge it to a reserve on the grounds that sooner or later a catastrophe will strike and huge claims will have to be paid. Rather than charging it all against income in the year the catastrophe occurs, these companies can use the reserve to cushion the blow. We are talking about big money here. According to Phillip Schwartz of the American Insurance Association, Hurricane Betsy in 1965 (when catastrophe reserves were unheard of) cost insurance companies $715 million in claims. Initial damage estimates for the tornadoes that swept the South and Midwest last April (all but obliterating Xenia, Ohio) exceed $1 billion.

With reserves a company can show a steady stream of earnings when the cash flow reality may be far different. This is known as "managing" earnings. Even today the stock market loves companies that show steady earnings growth; it still hates the cyclicals. Hypothetical example:

Company A's annual earnings look like this over three years: $1 a share; $1.10; $1.20.

Company B's earnings look like this: $1.20 a share; 80 cents; $1.30.

We don't have to belabor the point. Even though both companies have earned the same total amount over the three-year period, the market is almost certainly going to give company A the much better price/earnings ratio; it has the old magic in its earning curve. Never mind that the curve may be pure fiction. It's also pure gold. And yet the difference in the two patterns may have been achieved simply through the use of reserves. That is, company B took its beating the year it occurred. Company A spread it out.

Many of the insurance companies using catastrophe reserves are subsidiaries of conglomerates: Hartford Fire, of International Telephone & Telegraph; Fireman's Fund, of American Express; Home Insurance Group, of City Investing. Obviously, conglomerates have a strong interest in managing earnings where they can.

Understandably, mutual insurance companies have shied away. They don't worry about the stock market.

Companies making use of the reserves defend the practice. "I feel that *failure* to dampen fluctuations in earnings is misleading," says Paul Singer of CNA Insurance. "In *most* years, *most* companies experience less catastrophe loss than they should expect, and therefore report more profit on that exposure than they should. This is compensated for in occasional years when they suffer very large losses. Meanwhile, they present a rosier picture than stockholders can expect by undervaluing the risk the company is exposed to."

The proponents of the reserves argue that all premiums have built into them a provision for catastrophes. It is, therefore, only proper that part of premium income be set aside for the time when the catastrophe might occur. The smoothing of income is only incidental. "These reserves are more nearly the proper matching of revenue and related costs." argues Kenneth P. Johnson, a partner in Coopers & Lybrand and also a member of the American Institute of Certified Public Accountants' Accounting Standards Executive Committee.

Maybe so, but there are some points to consider. One is that the term "reserve" is somewhat misleading. "Reserve" is a good word; it sounds like conservative accounting, foresight, prudence, money squirreled away against a rainy day. In fact, however, it is simply a small bookkeeping shift; the money ends up under "reserves" rather than under "retained earnings." As far as actual assets are concerned, and actual cash flow, both the reserving and nonreserving company are in the same boat.

Between reserving and nonreserving, there is a third option: reinsuring. An insurance company can lessen its exposure by reinsuring part of its business.

Comes catastrophe and it loses less. We mean it *really* loses less. Unlike the reserving company, it does not suffer a cash loss that goes unreflected in its earnings statement. However, it also really earns less, since part of its premium income each year must be turned over to the reinsurer.

Complicated? Of course, but the point we are making is simple enough. The more you deal in reserves, the further you get from the real world of cash flow.

There is a basic principle involved here, and it extends well beyond the world of insurance accounting. Take the fairly common reserve for the expropriation of overseas assets. Here again, the intent is to guard against a sudden large loss in one year due to expropriation. As with catastrophe reserves, the reserve is not aimed at any particular event. Those favoring them say that history has shown that a certain portion of overseas assets tends to be expropriated over a period of time; hence the reserve.

General Motors' annual report says its $142-million expropriation reserve has not been touched since it was set up in 1954. When asked about it, John Nelson, GM's director of accounting says: "We still say we need it, and we do review it every year."

Critics contend that expropriation reserves should only be set up, if at all, when expropriation is imminent. The AICPA, which supports this view, defines imminence as that time when a government advocating nationalization comes to power, threats are made, other companies' assets are expropriated or the company's assets are seized.

The third major reserve being considered by the FASB is the self-insurance reserve. This reserve is set up when a company opts not to insure an asset and instead sets up a reserve against the risk it takes. In effect, it insures itself. Shell Oil decided in 1971 that it was paying a large amount for not very much, and decided against insuring its offshore drilling rigs and many of its onshore facilities as well. Instead it set up a reserve. If an offshore rig is destroyed now, Shell has to pay all the costs of cleanup from any oil spill and the replacement of the rig. Yet, like other companies with self-insurance reserves, Shell does not disclose the existence or the size of the reserve. R.C. Thompson, controller of Shell, says the size of the reserve is not material, but that it will be disclosed next year. However, the existence of the reserve is material even if the size is not, since self-insurance may expose a company to a large liability.

Here again the issue is the smoothing of income. "I think the income statement ought to reflect a loss in the year it happens," says Philip B. Chenok, a partner of Main, Lafrentz & Co., and a member of Accounting Standards Executive Committee. "If a company makes the decision not to insure against a hazard that other companies *do* insure against, then having made that decision, the financial statements ought to reflect the results of the decision. The income statement of a company that takes out insurance and pays the premium ought not to look exactly like the company that doesn't take out insurance. There is a judgment being made here, and the financial statements of those two companies ought to reflect the difference in judgment."

The AICPA's main objection to reserves for future losses is the very fact that they are *future* losses. "Our problem is the timing of the charge," says the Accounting Standards Executive Committee's Richard Lytle. "We do not feel that you should set up a charge against this year's income for a loss that has not yet occurred."

The simple and unquestionable fact of life is this: Business *is* cyclical and full of unexpected surprises. Is it the role of accounting to disguise this unpleasant fact and create a fairyland of smoothly rising earnings? Or should accounting reflect reality, warts and all—floods, expropriations and all manner of rude shocks? ■

June 15, 1974

EPILOGUE: In March 1975, the Financial Accounting Standards Board issued Statement No. 5, "Accounting for Contingencies," which outlawed the use of catastrophe and almost all other kinds of reserves. Because it also prohibits corporations from most forms of self-insuring, many businessmen are dead set against Statement No. 5 (see, "So whaddya suggest?", this anthology's final selection). For this reason and because the SEC has told the FASB and the AICPA that Statement No. 5 does not adequately disclose many contingencies, the FASB has given a high priority to reviewing FASB No. 5.

In spite of any defects Statement No. 5 may possess, the ruling does demonstrate that the AICPA precedes the rest of the world in terms of setting accounting rules which present the best picture of economic reality. If you don't believe it, just try understanding the annual report of a French, German, or Japanese company. Almost impossible! Or better yet, just read the following article in which American accountants receive far higher marks than their overseas counterparts.

Tower of Babel

Recently we were chiding an executive at Daimler-Benz, maker of Germany's famed Mercedes-Benz automobiles, about the seemingly greater profitability of our own General Motors. Replied the executive with a knowing smile, "We do not show all we have. You must look at the *Ruckstellungen*."

Ruckstellungen means reserves. And sure enough, right there on the liabilities side of the balance sheet was the item (thoughtfully translated into English) "Other Reserves." These, explained a footnote, covered "warranty obligations, etc." They were huge ($220 million) and growing. In fact, the company cheerfully admitted, they were Daimler-Benz' hedge against a downturn in world motor markets. But they also make profitability comparisons with a U.S. company unreal at best.

It's as if General Motors were to have said in 1973: "We earned $8.34 a share but we're only going to report $6 a share; we'll throw the other $2.34 into a reserve because 1974 doesn't look too good." Had General Motors done that, it would have been able to show a profit of something like $5.60 in 1974 instead of the depressed $3.27 it actually showed. That would have done wonders for GM's earnings curve. However, it wouldn't have helped General Motors with Internal Revenue, which won't permit this kind of reserve as a tax deduction. And it would have gotten the company in deep trouble with the Securities & Exchange Commission, which believes in realism, not symmetry.

But that is just about what Daimler and many other major European companies do. They like things to be neat. They don't like the wild swings that are typical of what the Continentals call "the Anglo-Saxon zone."

Another example: The German chemical giant Farbwerke Hoechst shows a reserve against price increases, among other things. In Sweden, where reserves kept back from tax are a way of life, telephone equipment maker L.M. Ericsson has both special inventory reserves and reserves for future investments. French chemical producer Rhone-Poulene has "provisions" of a vaguely identified nature—provisions that come to $120 million in a consolidated balance sheet two years ago. Even Holland's Philips Lamp, one of the best reported companies on earth and a leader in inflation accounting, lumps its pension fund provisions with "sundry provisions," explaining only that these "do not relate to specific assets; they are formed to meet commitments and risks connected with the course of the business."

Are such reserves a good thing? Depends on your point of view. Sir Henry Benson is British senior partner of Coopers & Lybrand and chairman of the recently formed International Accounting Standards Committee. He says, "No, definitely not." It is against the whole thrust of modern accounting, says Sir Henry, "because insofar as the profit-and-loss concept is concerned, you don't know what the true position is."

The U.S. representative to the IASC, Peat Marwick Mitchell partner Joseph Cummings, agrees. Continental accounting "is not to the benefit of investors," he said at a January meeting of the IASC in London. "Where financial statements have not been prepared for investors but for closely knit groups, there has been an interest in being more conservative." By closely knit groups Cummings means the banks that dominate European corporate financing, as opposed to the highly developed equity markets of the U.S. and Britain. And "conservative," in this context, means a setup designed to minimize taxes and smooth earnings, which requires setting up reserves in good times to be drawn down in bad. Such reserves are flatly prohibited in U.S. accounting.

Reserves aren't the only area of difference between accounting in the U.S. and abroad. In many countries, the financial results of affiliated companies are not combined. Therefore, since intra-company sales are not eliminated, a parent company can show a large profit by loading up an unconsolidated subsidiary with high-priced merchandise. Then there are those special charges and credits that in the U.S. might be classed as extraordinary items, but that would always be disclosed and explained. These are sometimes hidden in an overseas income statement under "other expenses" without elaboration.

But the reporting of reserves, at least, will change shortly because the IASC has issued its first ruling: that the accounting policies used in an annual report must be disclosed. Elementary, you say? It is not yet required by law in France; and while in Japan you must disclose, you need not do so in the annual report.

Then the IASC moves into tougher territory, in two standards proposed to take effect at the start of 1976. One, standardizing the valuation and presentation of inventories, would prohibit the kind of reserves that used to be hidden in inventories (though not necessarily the use of "rainy day" reserves). The other would give international investors the kind of consolidated figures they now get from U.S. and British firms. The consolidation standard has brought few cheers from the Europeans.

In fact, sniffs Krafft von der Tann, Germany's representative on the IASC: "This whole IASC is an effort of the Anglo-Saxon zone."

But if the Germans, French, Dutch, and Japanese (plus European associate members Belgium and Greece) are so cool to the IASC, why did they join with the Anglo-Saxons—the U.S., U.K., Canada, and Australia—at all? "Because you cannot afford to be out of the Anglo-Saxon zone," answers von der Tann. "It is that simple. Questions would be asked. We cannot have discrimination against German or French companies in international financial markets."

But the Anglo-Saxon accountants are not going to have it all their own way. "It's not going to be 'You have to do it our way or we won't play,'" says Philip Defliese, managing partner of Coopers & Lybrand. "It's not that kind of a game."

It could, however, turn into a surprising game for U.S. companies. An important item on the IASC agenda is inflation accounting, on which a final ruling is scheduled for April 1976. While the Financial Accounting Standards Board is only thinking about inflation accounting for U.S. companies, many Dutch companies are already using it. A handful of them have in fact adopted an extreme form of inflation accounting: Philips Lamp, for example, values its inventory and fixed assets on the replacement value or current cost basis, and depreciates its fixed assets accordingly, though this has reduced its reported earnings sharply.

If the IASC adopted the Dutch replacement-cost approach and could make it stick, companies all over the world could see their earnings drop dramatically because of huge hikes in depreciation charges, since replacement costs have skyrocketed. Dow Chemical, for example, estimates that its nearly $1-billion capital budget for 1975 is merely the equivalent of $500 million spent in 1970. Under a replacement-cost approach, depreciation charges would soar because they would be based on replacement cost, not on historical cost. Think how this would decimate the earnings of capital-hungry companies. (On the other hand, it would improve the "quality" of the earnings and might persuade investors to put higher price/earnings ratios on the stocks.)

If U.S. companies ever came to inflation accounting, they would probably want to issue a parallel report showing earnings under the old system at the same time. And the Europeans, while kicking the reserves habit, might end up reporting in several different ways, too. The final result might be better information for the investor. But the first result would be confusion compounded. The German, Krafft von der Tann, has a point when he says: "Ha! They talk of inflation accounting. We are suffering from an inflation of regulation: local regulation, EEC force statements, the SEC and U.S. accounting bodies—and now the IASC." ∎

March 15, 1975

# Excess capacity?

The accountant-client relationship has been likened to that of doctor and patient, priest and penitent, or even husband and wife. Do you haggle with your doctor over his fee, with your wife over the price of her birthday present? Of course not. Nor with your high-toned accountant over his bill. Accounting fees are just not discussed in polite company.

Such niceties are still the rule in corporation-auditor relations, but not in the hotly competitive municipal accounting field. Municipalities *must* make public information about audit contracts. Thanks to a 1976 amendment to the Federal Revenue Sharing Act, which forces local governments to undergo audits, the veil of secrecy surrounding accounting fees has been lifted somewhat. Surprise! Accounting fees aren't quite as haggle-proof as the profession would like you to think.

The soap companies call it "cents-off deals," department stores, "traffic builders." In accounting it's called "practice development." But price-cutting is price-cutting, no matter what you call it.

Among the Big Eight accounting firms, fees range as high as $100 an hour for auditing services. Nonnegotiable? Coopers & Lybrand is auditing the City of Boston for $500,000, about $7 an hour, and the State of Maryland for $587,000, less than $10 an hour. Venerable Ernst & Ernst, [now Ernst & Whinney] lost the Boston job with a bid of $397,000 because the city fathers felt the firm did not understand the scope of the job. But E&E won the State of New Hampshire auditing contract for that same amount, beating out bids as high as Deloitte Haskins & Sells' $555,000.

This kind of price-shaving takes its toll. Already it has cut into the average partner's take, causing a decline in partners' income at Coopers & Lybrand and Touche Ross. Peat Marwick Mitchell & Co., too, has seen margins sliced.

But why cut prices? After all, if accountants sit tight the business will probably come to them anyhow. The laws say the work *must* be done. The word from the CPAs is that they feel they are gaining expertise in the municipal audit field. But, notes Earl C. Keller, professor of accounting at the University of Michigan, audit rules are the same for cities and corporations. "All the CPA firms want to get larger," he says. "The corporate business is not expanding, all they're doing there is trading clients."

What do the accountants say? William J. Raftery, director of government services at Main Lafrentz & Co., is frank: "You have to have [spare] staff on hand for larger clients. We [accounting firms] wind up with excess capacity and, just like the Japanese dump steel, you could say there's some dumping of staff." His counterpart at Coopers & Lybrand, James A. Hogan, agrees: "Municipal jobs often come up during accounting's slow season—most fiscal years end June 30—so the people working on a lot of these jobs would be sitting around doing nothing if they didn't have the city audits to occupy their time."

As the municipal market battle continues—and for the first time ever the battle is in the open—some corporate clients are wondering why it's only cities that benefit from price-cutting. They are wondering if they aren't paying some of the cost of municipal audits.

"I suppose there's some social good," says Control Data Corp. comptroller Gary E. Polaczyk, "and from our viewpoint, it's okay as long as it doesn't go too far. If they're undercutting too much, obviously somebody's paying for it."

CDC's auditor, Peat Marwick Mitchell, audits the City of New York for $1 million a year—around $26 an hour. That is fairly high for a city job, but corporate audit committees across the country would drool at such a cheap contract. ■

June 25, 1979

3 FINANCIAL REPORTING OF CORPORATE ASSETS

Words can be deceiving. Take "asset." It suggests concrete wealth—money in the bank, oil in the ground, machinery in place and primed to create more wealth. But legion are the investors and creditors who have found air and confusion where they thought they would find solid wealth. You see, there are these fundamental problems with assets: Just what *are* they? and, Just what are they *worth*? The accountants debate incessantly over these critical questions.

As you may well conclude from the articles in this section, there are probably fewer ways to skin cats than to assign values to assets. Is the value of an asset its original (i.e., historical) cost? Is it the historical cost marked up over the years by changes in the general price level? Should "value" be the cost of replacing the asset? Or should it be measured by the price that the market at any given time is willing to pay?

Right there you have four fundamentally different ways to measure the worth of an asset. And what if two or more measurement schemes conflict? What happens, for example, if an acquiring firm pays more for an acquired firm's assets than the current fair market value of those assets? Answer: A new asset called "goodwill" or "excess purchase price" has been created.

There is nothing tangible about this asset. When hustling entrepreneurs built huge-but-flimsy balance sheets out of goodwill during the go-go years of the late 1960s, the accountants argued bitterly about how to account for all the new goodwill. They eventually compromised and decreed that goodwill must be amortized—that is, written off the balance sheet—within 40 years. This is a long time for a shaky asset to sit on a balance sheet. Besides, does such amortization get a true asset value? Before you say yes, read the article about the trouble radio and TV station owners have with goodwill ("When goodwill is bad news," page 63). And if you still aren't confused, read "Gimmick for all seasons," (page 66). a story about *negative goodwill* which reveals how quick-witted businessmen can make considerable financial hay by buying assets at less than their historical-cost-measured book values. (Unless American stock market prices rise substantially, we may well be hearing a good deal more about negative goodwill in the years ahead.)

Also in this section are articles dealing with capitalization—the question, that is, of which business costs should be deducted from income and which should be put on the balance sheet and called "assets." Are executive salaries "assets"? At least one company thought so. Are the costs incurred to find and dig worthless holes in the ground "assets"? Many oil and gas producing companies think so—and with better reason than you might expect.

And you thought "asset" was a straight-forward word!

Much ado
about nothing

Third down and long yardage. Deep in Jets territory. Namath, fading back, looks downfield. Then—the bomb!

That's what it felt like initially to the members of the Financial Accounting Standards Board when they fired off their first exposure draft on marketable securities in November after just 60 days' labor. A quick, bold stroke that would erase all those years of fumbling with the controversial question of portfolio valuation by the old Accounting Principles Board!

In a matter of days, however, the accountants were rudely awakened. There was no receiver downfield. And when they brought out the yardsticks on the final version of the FASB marketable securities exposure draft last December, it was a flimsy patchwork of compromise, loopholes and exceptions that amounted to no gain.

The whole affair illustrates the difficulty of trying to reduce financial reports to anything like precision. In the opinion of a good many businessmen and accountants, the whole proposal made things worse, not better. Typical was the initial response of John Skipper, vice president and top financial officer of fat-portfolioed Leaseway Transportation. "If you think we have a credibility gap with investors now," he said, "this proposal would just about take it *all* away!"

Huffed American Express' management, "It's unbelievable that, to avoid a minor audit difficulty in appraising impairment of value, steps would be taken to reduce substantially incentives to own equities at a time when there is unanimous judgment that this country needs trillions of dollars of capital."

Such reactions were as predictable as they were vehement. For so-called "float companies" like American Express, Sperry & Hutchinson, and Blue Chip Stamps of Time, Inc. and Leaseway Transportation, whose businesses typically generate large amounts of up-front cash floats that are invested in securities, the initial FASB draft would have had an enormous impact on reported earnings—cutting them sharply in the bear market of 1974, and boosting them sharply in the rally of 1975. Many large conglomerates would have been similarly affected.

What the long bomb from the FASB sought to force most companies to do was to mark equity investments to the lower of cost or market—immediately and retroactively. In the past, companies had the option of treating their equity investments either as current assets, carried at the lower of cost or market, or as noncurrent assets, carried at cost until sold. Thus, if the price of a particular stock fell below cost, some companies (notably Signal Cos.) were reluctant to charge the difference to earnings, and instead simply switched it from current to noncurrent status. The draft would have ended the switches.

Whose Ox Was Gored?

American Express reported earnings gains of from 3 percent to 6 percent for the first three quarters of 1975, for example. If the FASB's original draft had taken effect, those gains would have ranged from 51 percent to 72 percent. The travel services of American Express, which report publicly, would have shown a 354 percent increase in one quarter instead of just a 30 percent increase.

Over at Leaseway, the FASB draft would have chopped 28 percent off of 1974 earnings, and then added 21 percent to 1975's nine-month results. Per-share earnings at S&H would have been cut from $1.35 to 72 cents in 1974, but increased 25 percent for the first nine months of 1975.

Conglomerates like International Telephone, Gulf & Western, Loews, and Transamerica also would have been whipsawed. Had ITT's Harold Geneen been forced to mark down his big equity portfolio to market in 1974, he would have had to chop earnings by $177 million. Then by November 1975, he could have added most of that back. Transamerica's 1974 annual report disclosed the unrealized losses that appeared in the income account in a parenthetical statement. Its $39 million in earnings would have been largely wiped out by $44 million in unrealized pretax losses. In 1975, however, the reverse would have been true.

What on earth was the point of injecting such wild swings into reported earnings when everyone knew that eventually those equity investments would recoup their losses? So argued the companies with the fat portfolios. Actually the idea came from a committee at the American Institute of Certified Public Accountants in the depths of the 1974 bear market when the portfolio assets of many companies were worth hundreds of millions less than their reported cost value. In addition, the Securities & Exchange Commission issued Accounting Series Release No. 166 in December 1974, which called for greater disclosure of security gains and losses and "suggested" that the FASB consider the question of securities valuation.

By the time the FASB got around to it one year later, says George Catlett, a partner of Arthur Andersen and a former member of the now-defunct Accounting Principles Board, the problem had simply gone away. "There is nothing currently pressing about the marketable securities problem," says Catlett. "In 1975 the market was up."

That, of course, is precisely why the old Accounting Principles Board did nothing about portfolio valuation after extensive hearings in 1971. That problem seemed to go away too.

So the stage was set for compromise. Predictably, the compromises that followed pleased few and angered many. "In several critical accounting areas, the initial FASB exposure draft went from at least a *somewhat* tenable theoretical position to several untenable positions in their final statement," says Arthur Andersen's Catlett. "It's now a hodgepodge of accounting theories. The unintended result could well be further confusion."

That's putting it mildly. For one thing the final FASB statement continues to overlook some regulated industries where specialized accounting is used, like mutual life insurance. But it *does* apply in some cases to the consolidated statements of conglomerates that own insurance companies. The statement covers savings banks and savings & loan associations. Yet it *excludes* nonprofit enterprises like university endowments.

Nor does the statement apply to all equity securities. It applies to common stocks, warrants, rights and options, plus *some* preferred stocks. But any preferred stock that is redeemable, including convertibles, is excluded. Bonds that are convertible into common stock are also excluded.

Why didn't the FASB come to grips with the main question: How to value *all* marketable securities? "We realized that if we didn't narrow the scope to equity securities we couldn't get anything resolved in time for 1975," says the FASB's J.T. Ball, director of emerging problems. "We felt that the equity valuation problem was more pressing and, besides, it didn't involve breaking major new theoretical ground."

Costly Compromise

Having shied away from "breaking major new theoretical ground," however, the FASB wound up perpetuating existing problems. When, for example, should a common stock be listed as a current asset and when as a noncurrent asset? The FASB statement ducked the question. Perhaps because the distinction is meaningless to start with.

Clearly, however, whether a common stock is a current or a noncurrent asset can make quite a difference on the income statement of the company that owns it. Gains or losses in value on a current asset are credited or charged to net income. But gains or losses in value on a noncurrent asset are credited or charged to stockholders' equity, bypassing the income statement altogether. The second is the type of accounting practiced by most insurance companies who run gains or losses on equity securities through "surplus." "What the FASB wound up doing," says Catlett, "was to put *everyone* on the insurance 'to surplus' approach. That sets us back years in accounting."

It is also a step backward in consistency. Convertible bonds are marketable securities, for example. They change in value every day just as common stocks do, although usually to a lesser extent. Why should they be treated differently? Or what about mortgages, which are also marketable and constantly changing in value? By mandating special treatment for one type of marketable security, the FASB has simply undermined the meaning of corporate income statements.

What's more, 1975 income statements and balance sheets will not necessarily be comparable with 1974, because the FASB dropped its requirement for retroactive restatement.

Says one smiling financial officer, "The FASB may have scored early, but we won the game." ■

February 1, 1976

All numbers
are not equal

Our journey into the murky realm of significant uncertainty began innocently enough. We were leafing through *The Wall Street Journal* one bright morning last month, over a second cup of coffee, when a headline caught our eye: "Boothe Computer Auditors Give Firm A Qualified Opinion."

We knew Boothe Computer was having trouble; many independent computer leasing outfits have since IBM came out with its new System 370 computer line in 1970. Just weeks earlier Boothe had warned that its 1972 annual report would show a $36.5-million write-off of additional depreciation on its now-harder-to-rent portfolio of IBM 360 equipment. The write-off gave the company a $36.5-million loss for the year ($17.16 per share) and all but wiped out its net worth.

Now we read that even with the decks thus cleared, Boothe's auditing firm, Touche Ross & Co., had still qualified its opinion of the company's 1972 statements. A qualified opinion is no laughing matter. It's like tacking a quarantine notice up on a company's door. Bankers, creditors, beware! Bondholders, stockholders, on your guard! Touche Ross was saying that even with the carrying value of Boothe's rental equipment pared way, way down by the write-off, it still had serious reservations about the company's ability to recover the remainder of its computer investment through future rentals.

As we thought about Touche Ross, we remembered something else: that earlier this same auditing firm had given two of Boothe's biggest competitors in leasing IBM 360s—Leasco Corp.'s leasing subsidiary and Greyhound's 74 percent-owned Greyhound Computer Corp.—completely clean bills of health on their 1972 statements. In these cases, Touche Ross had furnished the standard two-paragraph " . . . in accordance with the generally accepted auditing standards . . . presents fairly, etc . . . " that gladdens the hearts of bankers and security analysts.

That piqued our curiosity. At a glance, all three computer leasors look pretty much alike: The same rental equipment, mostly IBM 360 gear. The same-sized rental portfolios, between $200 million and $260 million at original cost, grossing between $35 million and $60 million a year. The same overriding competitive factor, namely IBM, with its new 370 line and its troublesome new pricing policies announced during the last two years. Also, much the same accounting policies. All depreciate their 360 equipment in the U.S. on a straight-line basis over ten years (though Leasco and Greyhound figure on a 10 percent salvage value at the end, while Boothe is writing its equipment down to zero).

About the only visible major difference we could see was that Leasco's and Greyhound's computer leasing operations are relatively small parts of large companies, while Boothe's computer leasing revenues make up 80 percent to 90 percent of its total gross.

So how come Greyhound and Leasco got away with clean opinions for 1972, while Boothe, even after swallowing a big write-off, got a dirty opinion? We emptied our coffee cup and went digging for the annual reports.

Touche Ross' qualified opinion hit us first off when we opened Boothe's report. True to his maverick form, founder-chairman D.P. Boothe Jr. had put it right up there on page one for everyone to see. In substance, it said Touche Ross was not only worried about whether Boothe could recover its computer investment. It was also worried about Boothe's ability to maintain adequate financing (since its net worth had been written down to just $2 million) and about prospects for two small, but now quite crucial, subsidiary companies.

In the report itself, D.P. Boothe was very frank about all this. He concluded that even after writing this rental equipment down from $146 million to $90 million in 1972, his company would do no better (nor worse) than break even on computer leasing over the next five years.

Then we hauled out Leasco's and Greyhound's annual reports. In separate audits of their leasing operations, as well as the parent companies, Touche Ross had given both clean opinions. Both annual reports cited the hard times caused by the 370 and IBM's new pricing policies. Both conceded they were having a much, much harder time remarketing and extending 360 leases (which typically run from one to three years and are cancelable). Both conceded, too, that their computer leasing profits would decline in the future. But neither said anything about a profit washout, as Boothe had.

Why was Touche Ross relatively gentle with Leasco and Greyhound? Had Touche Ross reached into the way-beyond and attested to Greyhound's and Leasco's marketing forecasts? Why were these forecasts more optimistic than Boothe's? If they had approved the forecasts, was that a proper thing for an auditor to do?

By now we were itching to get in touch with Touche Ross. But first we wanted some more facts. How much of each company's 360 equipment still remained to be recovered? Boothe was now carrying its 360s at just 43 percent of original cost. But Leasco still had 60 percent to recover and Greyhound 57 percent. Score one for Boothe, it seemed to us.

And what about each company's progress in remarketing and extending leases? Boothe had turned over leases on equipment worth $141 million (at original cost) during 1972, or about 68 percent of its entire equipment portfolio. That may have fallen short of Boothe's lease expirations, but it indicated nonetheless that Boothe still had plenty of marketing muscle.

Then we wondered about the percentage of equipment off-lease—that is, how much was gathering dust in each company's warehouse collecting no rent? Boothe said it had 5.3 percent of its portfolio idle at the year's end (though D.P. Boothe later admitted to us it has climbed to 8 percent or so recently). By contrast, Greyhound had 11.3 percent off-lease at the end of 1972. Leasco bragged that it had no equipment at all off-lease—causing us to wonder about what kind of price concessions it was making. Furthermore, a footnote to Leasco's annual report warns that leases for computers costing $129 million remain to be renewed in 1973, or 50 percent of its portfolio. That's one-third more than Leasco renewed in 1972. It looked like still another point for Boothe, or at least a fraction of a point.

So there were serious uncertainties in Leasco's and Greyhound's futures as well as in Boothe's. More serious in some cases than Boothe's, it seemed.

Briefly, an unpleasant thought crossed our mind. Did greater size—and more specifically, the size of the auditing fee—have something to do with Leasco and Greyhound receiving clean opinions from Touche Ross? As we said, Touche Ross audited the leasing operations of both. But it audited the parent companies as well. And both parent companies are far larger than Boothe. Leasco, with Reliance Insurance as its fiscal backbone, has total revenues of $654 million, ten times more than Boothe. And Greyhound, with revenues just under $3 billion, is about 50 times larger than Boothe. Clearly, it was time to put some questions to Touche Ross.

Our adventure with Touche Ross is a story by itself. Suffice it to say, we went through three senior partners of the firm, including Board Chairman Robert Trueblood, before a New York-based partner named Robert Kay took a cab across town (in the midst of a driving rainstorm) to see us.

We told Kay what we had discovered and said it looked to us like the big guys come off better than the little guys. All three leasing operations had been audited separately, but it appeared to us that the two owned by bigger outfits got better treatment. "Well," he replied, "size did make a difference, but not the way you are implying. The big companies are naturally able to make a greater commitment of resources, both money and talent, to remarketing and extending their leases. Not just in the area of salesmanship, but in technical things too, like expanding the memories of their 360 equipment to make them more like 370s. When we looked at the size of Boothe, and the effort it was making in that area, there were significant uncertainties—not only in our minds but in theirs too."

So then, Touche Ross *had* attested to more than just balance sheets and income statements. Yes, replied Kay. "It boiled down to an evaluation of a forecast. But let me ask you where you draw the line? Isn't every auditior's opinion to some degree based on the assumption—in effect, the forecast—that the company in question will be able to remain in business for some period into the future?"

Sure, we said, to some degree. But what about that term, significant uncertainty? Aren't there significant uncertainties in Greyhound's and Leasco's computer leasing futures too? Sure, said Kay. "Uncertainty is the name of the game in computer leasing, where everyone is loaded up with short-term, cancelable leases. Significant uncertainties at Leasco and Greyhound must be recognized."

So, how come they got clean opinions? Or weren't forced to make write-offs? Answered Kay: "In their cases, we did not think the significant uncertainties constituted abnormal risks. But in Boothe's case there were interrelated significant uncertainties." He went on to explain that Boothe, after taking the big write-off, had reduced its net worth so much as to fall into technical default on some of its debt (though it has been granted an extension by the banks until the end of 1974 to clean up its financial situation). The second interrelated significant uncertainty was that two of Boothe's key remaining businesses—a computer terminal company and an airport equipment company—were also operating in the red. Boothe, in short, was really up against it.

Kay leaned across the table. "Look," he said, "if Boothe doesn't make it in this business, where does it go?" He paused to let that sink in. "Now this kind of consideration should never affect a company's accounting methods, and it hasn't in Boothe's case. But it sure can, and did affect the auditor's opinion.

"As I said before, we have in effect attested to these companies' marketing forecasts."

After parting company, we thought about what Kay had said. Touche Ross, with its eyes wide open, had wandered onto foreign ground in giving its stamp of approval largely on the basis of Leasco's and Greyhound's sales forecasts. Was it competent to make such judgments, involving marketing and technical expertise as well as accounting savvy? Was it proper?

Other auditing firms, such as Peat Marwick Mitchell and Arthur Andersen, have established tough, strictly numerical guidelines for dealing with computer leasing companies. They do examine forecasts, but they are more likely to force write-offs and consider giving dirty opinions. Touche Ross, says Kay, prefers to take it on a more flexible, company-by-company basis. Indeed, Touche Ross got the Boothe Computer account in 1972 when Arthur Andersen threatened to qualify its opinion for that year. Interestingly, Touche Ross is no longer looking for more computer leasing clients. As Kay put it: "We have enough problems in that business as it is."

As for us, we could only conclude that Touche Ross would have done us all a greater service if it had explained in more specific detail exactly what it was that it was certifying—that all three companies face significant uncertainties, but that in its opinion Boothe's uncertainties are more significant. Shareholders would not assume, as they may have by the absence of write-offs and dirty opinions, that Leasco and Greyhound are home free in computer leasing. ■

July 1, 1973

EPILOGUE: In mid-1978, the AICPA's Auditing Standards Executive Committee (AudSec) proposed that qualified opinions by CPAs be scrapped. The basic rationale: That under FASB Statement No. 5, there already is adequate disclosure of contingencies; thus qualified opinions are, according to the AICPA, redundant. But under pressure from the SEC's acting Chief Accountant Clarence Sampson (who told the AICPA "they'd better look more closely at FASB No. 5"), and from Big Eight accounting firms Arthur Andersen & Co, and Price Waterhouse & Co., the AICPA's AudSec quietly dropped the proposal. (For more on the issue, see "Lower the red flag? " FORBES, June 12, 1978.)

Physician,
heal thyself

Capitalize the president's salary? Even Teleprompter's own officers wouldn't buy its brand of free-wheeling accounting.

Cable TV may still live up to its advance billing as the major growth industry of the decade. But right now TelePrompTer, the AT&T of cable, with 143 systems and 900,000 subscribers scattered from coast to coast, would settle for a plainer, healthier and less dramatic future.

Its troubles stem from a $100-million construction program spread over the past two years—a huge load for a company with only $61 million in annual revenues. And construction was growing three times as fast as revenues. New York-based TelePrompTer, with twice as many subscribers as its nearest cable competitors (Tele-Communications and Warner Communications), was building new systems faster than it could pay for them. And the new systems weren't operating at a profit. (This year 24 systems became operational and generated operating losses totaling $1.8 million.) And accounting policies that heavily capitalized construction-related expenses masked the impact of what was happening.

The eventual revelation, which came after a nine-week stock trading ban imposed by the Securities & Exchange Commission, left TelePrompTer shares trading at a five-year low of $4.50, down from a high this year of $34.50. After reporting healthy first-quarter earnings of 24 cents per share, the company now expects the final 1973 figure to be only 12 cents, *vs.* 79 cents last year. Already there have been write-offs of $3.3 million. Disclosures made under SEC pressure show that of some $100 million TelePrompTer capitalized in the past year and a half, only $69 million clearly covers materials and labor costs. Another $27 million falls into nebulous payroll and expense designations that one analyst says "probably include even travel and entertainment."

You may remember TelePrompTer from 1971. That was the year former President Irving Kahn—now in federal prison—was indicted for bribery in an attempt to get a Pennsylvania cable franchise. Kahn, once head drum major for the University of Alabama, successfully tooted and touted TelePrompter—and with it much of the rest of the cable industry—to the point where the company's stock commanded a price/earnings multiple of 189 in the late 1960s. Those were the days when glamour concepts often sold for impressive multiples of capitalized losses.

In early 1972 Jack Kent Cooke, TelePrompTer's major stockholder, with 1.9 million shares, wrested control from the Kahn faction and brought in new directors and top management. The refurbished board included representatives of other big names with big blocks of TelePrompTer stock: Charlie Allen of Allen & Co.; Howard Hughes, who's in partnership with TelePrompTer in cable systems in New York City and Los Angeles; and Jack Wrather, the owner of broadcast rights to "Lassie" and "The Lone Ranger," who got a $25-million stock guarantee from TelePrompTer when the company bought the Muzak division of his Wrather Corp. in 1971.

After the takeover, Cooke stayed at his California ranch to mind his West Coast sports properties, the Los Angeles Forum and the Lakers and Kings basketball and hockey teams. He left operational control of TelePrompTer in the hands of Chairman and Chief Executive Raymond Shafer, a cable novice but former Pennsylvania governor who brought much-needed respectability, and President William Bresnan, a longtime Cooke employee with a background in small-town cable operations.

Soon there was a very different kind of whistle-blowing at TelePrompTer. In the spring of this year, Shafer hired two new financial men, brought in to replace Kahn regime holdovers. They were Bob Todd Jr., 41, who became vice president for finance, and Bill Trust Jr., 31, the new controller, both with banking backgrounds. Immediately they began to raise questions about TelePrompTer's policy of capitalizing much salary and overhead that related to construction. They calculated that about 30 cents of every dollar the company was capitalizing went for "people costs" and overhead that would not disappear even if the building stopped.

An internal struggle over corporate accounting policies ensued. All the while, says Cooke, 61, he was in intensive care on the West Coast recovering from a heart attack. "I wasn't even on the executive committee," he adds. Todd and Trust argued for a construction halt, write-offs and disclosure of the capital account. In 1972 TelePrompTer's annual report for the first time revealed that it was capitalizing construction interest. If that $3.2-million annual interest figure was significant enough to make public, Todd and Trust felt the company should also itemize overhead charged to the capital account and fully reveal its cash position.

Management didn't buy this thesis. TelePrompTer corporate officers argued that their own salaries should be capitalized, since they spent most of their time dealing with construction projects. One director warned that the company "shouldn't let these financial crepehangers slow down momentum."

During the summer TelePrompTer was operating in a negative cash position. From May to November it had gobbled up $102 million of a newly negotiated $150-million bank credit line. In mid-August things began to become unglued. TelePrompTer reported sharply lower earnings of 6 cents for the second quarter of 1973, citing operating losses from new systems, increased program origination and data processing costs as reasons for the drop. At the same time it boasted of continued construction.

After a crisis meeting—and under pressure from Todd and Trust—Tele-PrompTer on September 4 issued a press release announcing the suspension of $515 million in new construction. The financial men felt this wasn't enough. They thought the rising interest burden and the increasing rate of losses from new systems demanded a disclosure of the capital account's contents and a complete halt to work on the 22 systems being built.

On Friday, September 7, Todd and Trust—who by this time had their own outside counsel—called the SEC with their story. That evening the Commission suspended trading, and over the weekend Jack Kent Cooke, who had flown to New York, held an emergency board meeting at his suite in the Waldorf. Eventually Cooke, who acted with what he calls "a great sense of urgency," became chairman. "I sort of elected myself," he says. TelePromp-Ter subsequently made nine pages of additional accounting disclosures, and the trading ban was lifted November 12. A spokesman for the SEC says the Commission is still "actively investigating" the case.

Among the accounting revelations prompted by the SEC is the fact that the company really only *estimated* those construction labor costs that it capitalized in the first half of 1973. Those improper estimates now entail a $625,000 write-off. Similarly, TelePrompTer apparently miscalculated first half depreciation by $500,000. To top it off, the company recognized "anticipated profits" of $560,000 in its first half from two feature films produced by its Filmation subsidiary. Critics must have panned the pix, because the hoped-for profits got written off.

"We had a corporate animal so fat, so obese, so laden with lard that it couldn't move," explains Cooke. When he took over, TelePrompTer promptly dismissed over 900 of its 8300 employees and halted all construction. "In the past nine weeks," he contends, "we've trimmed off the excess fat."

Among the casualties were TelePrompTer's 21-man legal staff and a 5-man department that was assigned to locate new franchises; one man now handles franchises and there are no house lawyers. Heavy cutbacks may have eliminated the budgeted $4 million for local programing—once heralded as a prime public service benefit of cable. Also on the fiscal chopping block was data processing. The company ran a money-gobbling centralized computer billing operation for all its systems. Typically, many related expenses—even postage—showed up in portions of the capital account.

"The key questions," says Dennis McAlpine, an analyst for Tucker Anthony & R.L. Day, "are how much money did they save and how successful will their marketing be." The company must improve revenues and cut costs just to be able to service its debt of over $100 million. Also, there's still that $27 million of questionable capitalization that may have to be written off soon.

TelePrompTer cable systems now pass about 2 million homes, but the company has convinced only about 45 percent of those potential customers, 900,000 in all, to buy its services. With a staff of 451 commissioned salesmen, many newly hired, Cooke is now adding new customers at a rate of 23,000 a month, vs. 15,000 a month before he took over. But in order to draw more credit, the banks have imposed a year-end subscriber total on TelePrompTer that requires it to generate new business at almost twice its current rate.

Who's to blame for what went wrong? Shafer and Bresnan can legitimately claim defenses based on financial ignorance. "If Cooke had wanted a governor of Pennsylvania, he should have gotten Milton Shapp," says a Shafer associate. (Shapp, the state's current executive, is a cable millionaire who got $10 million for his stock in Jerrold Corp.—now owned by General Instrument—when he sold out in 1966.) "As for Bresnan, he's a terrifically nice guy, but basically a pole-climber who moved up the ranks," he adds.

Shafer says the difficulties resulted from rising interest rates, inflating costs of construction and legal commitments that had to be met to avoid losing franchises. "We were taking the necessary steps to get into a positive cash flow position."

"I think management thought like a construction company and not a cable company," says Cooke. "But I'm satisfied that on their own the staff would have defined the problems. They were becoming obvious."

TelePrompTer's accountant, Touche Ross & Co., won't comment. But Cooke now says he doesn't necessarily support the old accounting ways. "In the future we'll expense all we can," he indicates. On the other hand, says Shafer, "we were assured by the finest accounting people in the world that our policies were proper."

One bright spot that may emerge from the gloom is better accounting standards for cable TV. "Most cable operations—even the big ones—still have mom-and-pop financial mentalities," says Bowman Cutter, head of a Washington consulting organization. "But when you're all over the country like TelePromp-Ter, cash and capital budgeting controls aren't luxuries. With 143 operating centers, you run out of fingers pretty fast." Cable remains an excellent business in small towns, a run-of-the-mill business in middle-sized ones and a wretched business in big cities where construction costs are high and there's little additional programming cable can offer. TelePrompTer has some of each.

Meanwhile, Jack Kent Cooke—using the talent that made him Colgate-

Palmolive's leading soap salesman in his native Canada—keeps blazing away. He's recruiting a new, young management team and intends to stay at TelePrompTer until he finds a topflight man to run the company. "I like what the future holds, and have no intention of selling a share of stock," he says. No wonder. Cooke's estimated $40-million investment in the company is now worth less than $10 million. "There are a lot of people who can work miracles in business," he says. One would come in very handy just now. ■

December 1, 1975

EPILOGUE: After losing several million dollars in 1973, 1974, and 1975, TelePrompTer turned profitable in 1976; in 1978 the company earned approximately 75 cents per share. The price of the company's stock rebounded from less than $2 per share in 1975 to over $14 per share in 1978. It wasn't that Jack Kent Cooke found a miracle worker. What was discovered is that to be soundly profitable, a company needn't resort to accounting gimmicks such as labeling executive salaries "assets."

A legitimate fiction?

The trouble with FORBES readers is that they ask such difficult questions.

Several days ago, for example, we received a thoughtful letter, complete with charts, graphs and painstaking computations, from George W. Higgs of Arlington, Va.

How about trying to separate myth from reality in the earnings of electric utilities? he wrote.

Higgs, it seems, owns a few shares of Duke Power and Virginia Electric & Power. One day, while carefully perusing the 1972 annual reports of those two companies, he noticed that both derived most of their earnings from something called "allowance for funds during construction."

From what?

Oh, yes. That was the label given to capitalized interest charges on money borrowed to finance the construction of new generating facilities. The already highly leveraged utilities were having to expand furiously these days, tying up huge slugs of borrowed capital which wouldn't be producing a return for over five years—the time it frequently takes to build a generating plant. In many cases, charging the interest on that money to current earnings would really clobber earnings—and hence the ability of utilities to raise capital. So states permitted utilities to capitalize that cost of money while the plant was being built—spreading its cost over the life of the building like other construction costs. This produced a credit, an addition to current earnings, called "allowance for funds during construction" (let's call it AFC).

Trouble was, of course, some of that borrowed money was raised by selling common stock. Here the utility using AFC was allowed to report *now* the kind of earnings it hoped to show on that common stock equity in the *future*, after discussions with the state power commissions. We'd often wondered about that. *This* portion of AFC didn't seem to us to be much more than wishful thinking.

A good point. We read on.

Did we realize, reader Higgs wrote, that AFC accounted for some 87 percent of Duke Power's $58.5-million "balance for common" (net income after preferred dividends), and some 67 percent of Vepco's $85.2-million balance for common? That AFC was their most important source of earnings?

Now what about this AFC? asked Higgs. Was it *really* income? Did it make any sense that the more a company spent on construction, the larger its reported earnings?

It was a good question, all right.

Our search for an answer led us to a noted Wall Street analyst who, by good luck, had just finished a survey of 80 major utilities' accounting practices. (He asked to remain anonymous so he could speak frankly.)

According to figures supplied by the Edison Electric Institute, the major utilities derived an average of 29 percent of their balance for common from AFC last year. And that figure was rising steadily. In 1970, it was 20 percent. And back in 1965 it was only 4 percent.

Duke Power, at 87 percent, probably derived more of its 1972 reported balance for common from AFC than any other major utility in the country, reflecting an unusually big construction program, the analyst went on.

He had no quarrel with the concept that the cost of money is as much a cost of construction as is the cost of bricks and mortar, and hence could be capitalized and depreciated over the life of the building. The accounting theory seemed sound.

But then the analyst surprised us. Because Duke Power derived so much profit from this constructive fiction, he said, "this certainly lowers the quality of Duke's earnings."

Why, we asked, if the cost of money is a legitimate part of construction costs?

"Because of the regulatory lag," he replied. "The question is when will the state power commission allow them to earn a rate of return that justifies what they've been taking in AFC?—which, after all, is revenue that's going to be earned later."

Once Duke's generating plants are on stream, that portion of the AFC earnings stops. Given the steady inflation in money, construction and operating costs, the chances are Duke wouldn't be earning anywhere near as much on them as it had already reported under AFC. At least not until it took its next rate case to the public utility commission, and it could take a year or more for the commission to act. Result: a decline in Duke's earnings in the interim.

Electric utilities with less ambitious construction programs were often able to avoid such "lags" by means of new AFC credits from new construction projects. But not Duke—it was increasing capacity by 58 percent over the next 15 months.

In other words, we thought, the more rapidly a utility expands, the more difficult it becomes—during inflation—for rate increases to cover sharply increased construction costs. And, of course, the longer state power commissions postponed granting those rate increases the more costly it would be for the utility to continue financing the needed expansion. Again, assuming continued inflation.

Recently, we recalled, Georgia Power had had to cancel a major financing because the Georgia Power Commission hadn't granted a hoped-for rate hike. Without it, Georgia Power simply didn't have enough current cash flow to cover interest charges on its new financing. Its large AFC was probably of little help since typical utility mortgage restrictions permit only 15 percent of AFC to be used to cover interest payments.

Still somewhat perplexed, we decided to raise the question with one of the country's leading experts in public utility accounting, a man named Richard Walker, managing partner of Arthur Andersen's Regulated Industries division, and a veteran of 29 years in the field.

Walker stopped us the moment we mentioned Duke Power's 87 percent AFC.

Actually, he explained, to the extent that AFC reflected the cost of debt money, as opposed to equity money, shareholders needn't worry about it. The interest cost was just subtracted from reported income as a cost, and then added back as an AFC credit when it was capitalized. No addition to current reported earnings. The interest portion of construction costs should never have appeared on a utility's income statement in the first place, since it wasn't really a cost of operations for the period.

The cost of equity capital was an entirely different matter, Walker went on. Future earnings were, in effect, being shown as present earnings. There *was* an addition to current reported earnings. "Some of these utilities have a third or more of their capital tied up in construction for several years, being serviced by future credits," said Walker.

We thumbed quickly through Duke Power's most recent prospectus and found that the common stock portion of AFC represented 49 percent of Duke's *reported* 1972 balance for common. Each year it was 7 percent to 8 percent higher.

But Walker conceded that there was no current cash flow behind *all* 87 percent of Duke's reported AFC earnings.

Quite a liquidity problem, we remarked. Was there any solution?

"For those utilities that have a large portion of their assets tied up in construction," Walker replied, "and where so much of the earnings of common stock comes from this imputed return on common equity that shareholders feel the cash flow is inadequate, then I think the regulatory body ought to permit the utility to put all or part of its construction work in progress in its rate base and thus improve current cash flow through higher rates."

Some 30 state power commissions, including most recently New York State, had done this or the equivalent. But not the North Carolina and South Carolina power commissions regulating Duke Power, Walker continued. This was a mistake, he felt. Current customers of Duke Power should pay the carrying costs of at least a substantial part of that new construction in the form of increased rates, since they were getting the present value of knowing that their future power needs would be met.

Walker concluded, "Unless the state commissions commence to come to grips with this probelm—this concern of investors about liquidity—we may find that the entire structure of the utility industry is threatened by government intervention, because of the inability of private utilities to raise capital."

As we pondered all this wisdom, we still had no clear answer to our reader's question, which was: How real are utility earnings? Wasn't there something basically wrong with a situation where a company was forced to report somewhat questionable future earnings? Maybe the problem, then, wasn't really one for the accountants. It was one for the public service commissions and for the politicians and the public.

If commissions insist on being penurious with rate increases, if they try to force stockholders to absorb the burden of inflation, then the utility companies are going to have to resort to "creative" accounting to hide what is happening. In the long run the investor will catch on, and the flow of capital will dry up. Will politicians still be bragging about keeping utility rates down when the lights start going out?

Yes, reader Higgs, there is something not quite kosher with electric utility earnings. Only don't blame the accountants. ■

November 1, 1973

When goodwill
is bad news

One of the big problems of the accounting profession is that it must lay down general principles to deal with specific cases. The general principles, however, like ready-made suits, do not fit every specific case. That, in essence, explains the excitement now going on over the accounting requirement that intangible assets, especially goodwill, must be amortized.

Such intangible assets are a queer breed. Accountants define them as what you buy in a company if you pay more than the fair market value of the company's tangible assets—plant, machinery, inventory, land, receivables and the like. When high-stepping congolomerators of the 1960s paid outrageously in-flated prices for companies, the excess was called "goodwill." Using goodwill, hustlers created huge, often fictional asset growth with no corresponding penalty, since in those days the accountants did not require that goodwill be written off. It would sit on the asset sheet forever, looking impressive, but often worth nothing or less than nothing.

That abuse was finally outlawed in October 1970 when the accounting profession adopted Accounting Principles Board Opinion 17. It said *no* asset has an eternal life; therefore all intangibles, including goodwill, must be amortized. The amortization period set was 40 years.

A decent general principle, but it apparently does not fit all the specific cases. There has been an increasing outcry against it from a variety of com-panies—truckers, for instance, whose most essential possession is the Interstate Commerce Commission license (an intangible asset) that permits them to haul freight across state lines. And newspaper publishers, who insist that the most important things they buy, when they acquire a new paper, are the intangibles of an established name and circulation base.

Most seriously affected are the broadcasters. Here's why:

Take the case of New York-based Lin Broadcasting Corp. (1974 revenues: $26.5 million). In November 1974 Lin acquired KXAS-TV in the lush Fort Worth-Dallas market. Lin paid $35 million. Of that, only $11 million was assigned to KXAS's tangible assets. The other $24 million was paid for the station's Federal Communications Commission license and its lucrative NBC network affiliation, both intangibles.

This is common practice in broadcasting. When another broadcast company, Metromedia, bought a Chicago FM station for $2.8 million, a trivial $20,000 was assigned to tangible assets. The rest went for the FCC license and other intangibles.

Under Opinion 17, those intangibles must be charged to profits within the next 40 years. So the KXAS-TV deal will cost Lin some $600,000, or 26 cents per share, annually. Considering that Lin's 1974 per-share net was only 95 cents, that charge hurts plenty.

On top of it all, the Internal Revenue Service generally will not allow amortization of the intangibles as a deductible item for tax purposes. So, the penalty to earnings is equivalent to $1.2 million pretax, rather than just $600,000. "Put another way," says Arthur Andersen & Co. partner Charles Johnson, "a 40-year amortization period with no tax benefit is really only a 20-year write-off. That's what really hurts these companies."

The broadcasters agree that Opinion 17 is a good thing for stopping the abuses of conglomerators. But they argue that the broadcast industry is in a different class. Its intangibles are almost certain to increase in value, since the licensing system limits market entry. Michael O'Sullivan, Lin's controller, puts it this way: "These intangibles have continuing value, and I don't see why we should have to amortize them."

He has a point. Back in 1962 Lin bought three radio stations for $2.5 million, of which $1.8 million was for intangibles. Last May Lin sold the same three stations for $8.7 million to Multimedia Broadcasting Corp. Of that $8.7 million, Multimedia figures it paid $5 million for intangibles. So Lin's intangibles *increased* some 200 percent in value.

The industry also argues that Opinion 17 affects it far worse than other industries, since typically 60 percent of a broadcast company's assets will be intangibles. "One-fortieth of very little is very little," says Ron Irion of the National Association of Broadcasters. "But one-fortieth of a hell of a lot can be a hell of a lot."

Another inequity, claim some, is that the young and growing broadcast companies are penalized more than the industry giants like CBS or NBC, which purchased most of their stations before the rule went into effect. Thus, their amortization burden is much less than it is for the younger companies.

The companies apparently do have the support of many accountants. A special entertainment companies task force of the American Institute of

Certified Public Accountants recently wrote an opinion reaffirming the applicability of Opinion 17 to the broadcast companies. But according to Charles Johnson, an author of the draft, "When we got to the intangible assets, most of us were sympathetic with the industry."

Why, then, doesn't the AICPA provide some relief? No power, says Johnson, pointing out that only the Financial Accounting Standards Board can do that.

The FASB does have the whole matter of accounting for business combinations on its agenda. Michael Pinto, FASB member, agrees that the board feels the rules need re-evaluation. But when an opinion will come from the already overburdened FASB is anybody's guess.

The sooner the better. You can make the case that accounting should be aimed at ending abuses. But it should also reflect an accurate economic picture. For broadcast companies at least, Opinion 17 gives a faulty image. ■

November 1, 1975

Gimmick for all seasons

Why would a $336-million company with a fairly respectable 10.9 percent return on equity and very little debt want to seize control of an ailing, highly leveraged company more than twice its size that earns barely 5 percent on stockholders' equity?

We looked back at the morning paper: Emhart Corp. was tendering for another 1 million of USM Corp.'s 4.1 million common shares. Since Emhart had already acquired 1.24 million USM shares from Alleghany Corp. last year for $31 million, the new offer—if successful—would give it 54 percent of USM's outstanding common and 43 percent of its voting stock.

Obviously, Emhart wants USM—formerly United Shoe Machinery—badly. First it had tried a friendly merger that failed nine months ago. Then, to avoid antitrust problems that might cripple the new tender offer, Emhart had sold off one of its own subsidiaries, acquired years before from USM. But why? Why was USM, which sold as low as $12 earlier this year, worth $23 a share to Emhart?

Behind all the usual verbal smoke screen about complementary businesses (both companies make machinery, if that means anything), there usually is a financial advantage. The most obvious possibility is that Emhart thinks it can achieve a fast turnaround at USM once it has effective control. Given USM's long history of poor profitability and antitrust problems, however, such a turnaround would surely be a while coming.

A second possible attraction is access to USM's cash flow of close to $50 million, not to mention the cash that could be generated by selling off some of USM's assets. But along with that benefit would come USM's $171-million debt load. Not an unmixed blessing, obviously.

Then the light began to dawn. USM is a Super Loaded Laggard. Emhart is offering $23 a share, a nice premium over market, for stock with a per-share book value of $53!

Okay, but what's so hot about that? There are literally hundreds of Loaded Laggards around today. Some of them are fated to remain laggard for a long, long, time. If an ordinary investor buys one, he may well find his bargain pretty shopworn.

But it is different when another company buys a Loaded Laggard. For one thing, there's a good bookkeeping gimmick known as "negative goodwill." This is the difference between the price you pay for the company and its book value. There is a very blah difference for the smaller investor, but a very luscious one for the corporate investor.

No, under purchase accounting (when the company is acquired for cash instead of stock), the buyer can't take the difference between cost and book value into earnings, except under very special circumstances. Instead, the accounting rules require that the buyer write down the value of the noncurrent, noncash items (like plant and equipment) to the point where the book value equals the purchase price; the negative goodwill disappears.

But its consequences don't disappear. There still is a big bookkeeping advantage to the purchaser. Now that he has written down the value of the plant and equipment, he can reduce the amount of annual depreciation charges as well.

Take a simplified case. One company buys another for $500,000 when the book value is $1 million. Say $750,000 of that book value is in plant and equipment and these assets are being depreciated over ten years at straight-line rates. Annual depreciation charges: $75,000.

With the write-down, the plant and equipment is reduced to $250,000. Now the purchaser can cut depreciation charges to $25,000. The extra $50,000 a year he throws into income. Obviously cash flow isn't improved, but reported earnings are, and to some people that's worth plenty.

Let's take a sharp pencil and apply this principle to a possible takeover of USM by Emhart.

If Emhart's tender offer succeeds, it will own 54 percent of USM, enough to consolidate its share of USM on the books. For $54 million in cash it will own $119 million in book value. The *difference*—that is, the negative goodwill—is $65 million.

However, USM carries some positive goodwill worth $29 million on its books, arising from earlier acquisitions by USM. First, Emhart would have to wipe out its share of this goodwill—$15.5 million—leaving the new negative goodwill at just under $50 million.

We now subtract this new figure from Emhart's share of USM's total noncash, noncurrent assets, which amount to $104 million. We end up with a new value for Emhart's share of USM's physical assets of $54 million.

On USM's present books, depreciation charges last year came to $12.3 million on the 54 percent of the assets that Emhart would acquire. But after the write-down, depreciation would need be only $6.5 million.

By cutting depreciation charges by nearly $6 million, Emhart would increase its reported pretax earnings by $6 million or about $3 million after taxes. This is no one-time gain. It would continue until the day when USM's assets were completely depreciated. This move alone would have added about 50 cents a share to Emhart's earnings last year—on top of the nearly $2 a share it would gain from consolidating USM's originally reported profits—or an increase of almost 90 percent to Emhart's 1974 earnings. On an investment of $54 million, Emhart would have shown a return of $14.5 million—27 percent on its money. Pretty good!

Emhart is by no means the only company to have noticed the negative goodwill play. It could well be a factor in Crane Co.'s offer to pay $25 per share for 22.6 percent of Anaconda, which has a book value of over $57 a share. And in North American Philips' recently paying $9 a share for Magnavox with a per-share book of around $11.

Indeed, this may be only the beginning of what could be a new takeover wave. Just look at the number of well-known blue-chip companies selling for less than 50 percent of book value in "Loaded Laggards."

"The real gimmick today is purchase accounting," says Harvey Kapnick, managing partner of Big Eight CPA firm Arthur Andersen. "When you get negative goodwill, it tends to inflate earnings unrealistically and therefore it misleads the investor." Kapnick thinks the whole concept of negative goodwill— be it through direct amortization into income, or through reduced depreciation charges against earnings—should be scrapped. "The assets should be put on the books at their current value, regardless of whether the stock market is at a high point or not." Any difference, he continues, should be credited to stockholders' equity.

Sidney Davidson, dean of the Chicago Business School, scoffs at that. "I don't see how you can say that purchase accounting overstates earnings and understates assets. Harvey Kapnick says he knows the value of the assets better than the market does."

Temptation

But let's assume Emhart views USM as a sound long-term investment. If so, then Emhart should be planning now for the eventual replacement of USM's assets, particularly in an inflationary period when even current depreciation rates are inadequate for replacement.

But the accountants require that Emhart *reduce* the depreciation charges on USM's assets.

The obvious temptation is to run the acquisition into the ground.

Philosophically, you can make a good case that the purchase method is sound. The trouble is that not everybody is a philosopher. Purchase accounting will tempt some companies to take over others for no other good reason than to dress up their books and to liquidate the acquired assets. We don't know the answer to the problem, but we do see real potential for abuse in a badly depressed stock market like the present one. ∎

October 1, 1975

Can a dry hole
be an asset?

Here is a paunchy, middle-aged man. And here is a scrawny eight year old. Your assignment: Design one set of clothing that must fit both comfortably, and describe their profiles—accurately.

This, in effect, is the latest dilemma facing the Financial Accounting Standards Board. The FASB is under a mandate from the Securities & Exchange Commission (which in turn, is under pressure from Congress) to review rules sometime before the year's end telling the nation's oil and gas (and mining and pipeline) companies how to account for their hefty exploration costs.

"The FASB is faced with two differing philosophies without a heck of a lot of middle ground for any compromise that would make conceptual sense," explains Philip E. Smith, Houston partner with the Big Eight accounting firm of Arthur Andersen & Co. "So whatever the FASB does will make a lot of people awfully mad."

The strong emotions can be explained by the big money involved. Suppose a company spends $100 million to drill for oil. Most likely, 90 percent of the effort will turn up dry holes; the remaining $10 million worth will be associated with finding income-producing reserves.

The question is: Should the company use the so-called successful-efforts method? That is, write off the costs of its unsuccessful efforts against income immediately, and so recognize immediately that dry holes are not assets. Or should the company use the full-cost approach? In the latter, you capitalize the *entire* exploration cost, on the theory that finding nine dry holes is part and parcel of discovering one income-producing well. Profits and stockholders' equity will tend to be greater under the full-cost method than they would be under successful-efforts accounting. Why? Because all exploration expenditures, dry holes included, are capitalized as a necessary cost of the income-producing reserves. Thus all dry holes are booked as assets instead of being written off as a cost against income.

Most of the major oil companies want the successful-efforts approach to be standardized. While some majors do use full-cost for some of their operations, their feeling seems to be that successful-efforts is in general a superior accounting concept. "A dry hole isn't an asset, is it?" asks George Weed, assistant comptroller at Exxon. "So why capitalize costs associated with it?" Agrees Robert Ferst, the head partner at "Little Eight" accountants Laventhal & Horwath: "It's like going to the racetrack: If you lose on a given day, then under the successful-efforts method, you'd tell your wife: 'I lost.' But under full-cost, you'd tell her: 'I made an investment; lets wait a while to see whether I won or lost.'"

But the reason the whole thing is such a hassle for accountants is that smaller oil companies have a different viewpoint. The independents' argument is that exploration costs *are* an investment; they should *all* be associated with assets, and not expensed against income.

"You ask any oilman how a company really works," argues Michael August, vice president at Houston's $52-million (revenues) Inexco Oil, "and he'll tell you that he has to justify his *entire* exploration effort as a capital investment, even though he knows that maybe 90 percent will go for dry holes." It's true, of course, that the assets booked from exploration must be amortized over the life of the reserves—ten years, say. But for a growing company, the decline in reported expenses resulting from the capitalization of all exploratory expenditures more than offsets the increased amortization.

There is more to this debate than mere accounting concepts, however. The real issue, from the independents' viewpoint, is profits. They emphasize that since they spend relatively more of their income for exploration than the majors, their earnings will suffer drastically if they are forced to switch to successful-efforts accounting.

How drastically? Inexco's Mike August estimates that under successful-efforts, his company would have reported total profits of less than $10 million over the last six years. But by using full-cost, the company reported earnings of $28 million. In 1974 alone, full-cost profits were $2.4 million. Under successful-efforts, Inexco would have shown a $7-million *loss*.

Mesa Petroleum's founder and chairman, T.B. (Boone) Pickens, put the implication of this bluntly to the FASB last month. He told the Board that had he been forced to report minimal, even nonexistent, profis under successful-efforts, he could never have taken his company public in 1964, and so could not have raised the more than $150 million in cash necessary to grow from a $1.5-million-sales company in 1965 to one with revenues last year of $99 million. In an interveiw with FORBES, Pickens added: "If the successful-efforts approach wins out, it will be almost impossible for a young, growing company to get financing. And that will just cut out a great deal of competition within the industry."

The pipeline companies are worried, too. Like the independents, they are increasing their spending to find reserves. They fear that a forced move to successful-efforts would sharply increase their debt-to-equity ratios since equity is generally lower under successful-efforts. "These companies fear that their ratings will go down and their borrowing costs up," says Geoffrey Hertel, a petroleum analyst with Houston's Rotan Mosle Inc.

On the other hand, moving from successful-efforts could well reduce companies' returns on equity, since equity tends to be higher under full-cost. "I think that the major oil companies are missing a hell of a good political bet by supporting successful-efforts," says a small Texas oilman.

The major companies use successful-efforts accounting for historical reasons. Way back when most of their accounting systems were set up, oil was relatively cheap and easy to find; there was no special reason for them to want to capitalize costs of dry holes. Now they tend to want to stick to the old system for a variety of reasons, not the least of which is a reluctance to go through the expense and the bother of restating earnings and assets.

Some accountants, moreover, regard successful-efforts accounting as basically more honest. Laventhol & Horwath's Ferst argues that full-cost accounting can be more easily abused. He cites one client—unnamed—who has been using full-cost accounting for years, booking the dry holes as assets but not finding any oil to offset them. "We didn't *agree* to their using full-cost," says Ferst, "but what could we do? We have to go along with full-cost because it is in conformity with generally accepted accounting principles."

The fact is, the FASB may not be the final arbiter on the matter. Ferst says political pressure could well be the judge: "A lot of smaller, fast-growing companies could have real trouble financing their growth if successful-efforts accounting were made the standard. If things go against them, I can see a rash of letters going out to congressmen." You can almost hear the politicians using a successful-efforts decision as further "proof" that the majors are trying to drive the independents out of business.

Perhaps the FASB has a real opportunity here. Why not allow *both* methods, as the old Accounting Principles Board was about to do just before it was disbanded in 1973? No one likes the confusion that can be generated by alternative accounting practices, but the fact is, growing oil companies are structurally different from the mature majors. Trying to force them all to wear the same suit of accounting clothes could very well end up causing more confusion than it avoids. ■

May 15, 1977

EPILOGUE: Accountants are continually pressed to make accounting principles "uniform" that is, to eliminate alternative methods by which corporate managements can account for a particular economic event. With the exception of FASB Statement No. 8 (see section 6, starting at page 119), there probably has been no accounting issue responsible for more furor than how U.S. oil and natural gas producing companies should account for the costs accociated with drilling dry holes. Dry holes? They are the empty, economically worthless wells that oil and gas firms drill in the process of drilling wells that turn out to be "wet," or economically valuable, ones.

Should the companies be forced to account for dry hole discovery and drilling costs using one uniform method? And if so, which method should they use? Are dry holes assets whose costs should be capitalized on the balance sheet? Or are dry holes dead losses whose costs should be deducted from income immediately?

During 1976 and 1977 the FASB—pressed by the SEC which in turn was under pressure from Congress—pondered these questions. In December 1977, the board issued its ill-fated Statement No. 19, which required that all companies use the "successful-efforts" method—that is, firms should expense, not capitalize, dry hole drilling costs.

A major effect of Statement No. 19 was to reduce reported profits of the country's smaller oil and gas companies because they had often been capitalizing dry hole costs. So infuriated by Statement No. 19 were these small-but-politically-potent companies that they appealed, in effect, to their congressmen. Exactly what transpired behind closed doors in Washington is not known. But what ultimately happened is known. In August 1978, in hotly contested action, the SEC issued Accounting Series Release No. 253 and in so doing effectively overruled the FASB. By 1981 oil and gas producers, said the SEC, should drop *both* the successful-efforts and full-cost accounting methods and replace them with a new accounting technique, "reserve recognition accounting." Many experts believe reserve recognition accounting will prove impractical; even the SEC has its doubts. But powerless before the SEC, the FASB suspended its hard-wrought Statement No. 19 in October 1978.

Will reserve recognition accounting solve the problem or create more problems? Did the SEC overrule the FASB under pressure from senators and representatives? Has the stage been set for more SEC intervention in the FASB's affairs? We don't know the answers to these questions. But we do think they are among the most important questions facing the accounting profession.

You can't legislate accounting principles

Congress put the problem to the SEC, which put it to the FASB, which solved it in a way the SEC didn't like. So the SEC came up with its own oil and gas industry accounting rules, which could confuse and even seriously mislead investors.

"This new [Securities & Exchange Commission] rule just goes to show that when Congress tries to legislate accounting principles, chaos results. It's like trying to legislate poverty out of existence: Certainly a worthy objective but also a difficult thing to do."

That is Clifford E. Graese (pronounced "grace") speaking. Graese, 51, is vice chairman of the biggest of the Big Eight accountants, Peat Marwick Mitchell & Co. (1977 revenues: $516 million); he is a thoughtful man and not a knee-jerk government hater. Indeed, his profession would hardly be so lucrative were it not for the rules and red tape of Big Government. But Graese *is* agitated by the SEC's new proposal, Reserve Recognition Accounting, for how the nation's oil and gas companies should keep their books. "RRA goes too far too fast. It leads to a high degree of imprecision and uncertainty in the income statement and balance sheet."

Graese is not alone. Here's Harvey Kapnick, chairman of $500-million-plus (1978 revenues) Arthur Andersen & Co.: "Long run, it's a good idea, but initially it will cause difficulties. We'll have to develop significant new auditing standards. . . . Scary!"

Or listen to Donaldson, Lufkin & Jenrette, Inc. Managing Director John Chalsty, who has spent several years advising the government and the Financial Accounting Standards Board on accounting principles for oil and gas companies: "It's an incredibly complicated rule, and I have serious doubts that it can even be implemented."

Or Joseph Connor, Price Waterhouse's new chairman: "It's pretty frustrating that after FASB considered this matter so long, the commission opted instead for a radically new type of accounting that is highly subjective, untested and unproven."

Radical, subjective, unproved and untested accounting rules coming from the august SEC accountants?

Here's what all the flap is about:

Oil and gas companies have traditionally used one of two basic approaches to account for their exploration and production expenditures. Under one, the full-cost approach, a company capitalizes costs for *all* exploration, including the costs associated with dry holes. Full-cost accounting says, in effect, that dry holes as well as wet ones are assets, since to find the latter you also must find the former. The other approach, successful-efforts, says you capitalize only costs associated with wells that come in; dry-hole costs are written off against income immediately.

Result: Companies using full-cost tend to show higher earnings and accumulate assets faster than do companies using the successful-efforts approach.

The SEC never liked these alternative accounting systems. Late in 1975, the SEC and FASB agreed that the Board would arrive at one uniform method. The FASB sat down, produced a 400-page discussion memorandum, wrung its hands and last December produced FASB Opinion 19. It said: Only successful-efforts accounting from now on.

This upset the country's smaller oil and gas producers—and, unlike the FASB, independent oilmen have plenty of political clout. They used it to the extent that Congress itself almost overturned the FASB when the Haskell amendment was narrowly defeated. To the independents' rescue: the SEC.

On August 29, in a highly unusual personal appearancce to usher in an accounting proposal, SEC Chairman Harold Williams announced that the commission found *both* successful-efforts and full-cost accounting inadequate "because neither reflects the economic substance of oil and gas exploration in a meaningful manner." The SEC, said Williams, found a third and even better way: Reserve Recognition Accounting, or as the trade already calls it, RRA. In the spirit of the times, RRA is extraordinarily complex: The rule itself runs to 200 pages and Chairman Williams needed another 13 pages to introduce it. Few people have read it and even fewer digested it. But if the SEC has its way, oil and gas company stockholders had better get used to RRA if they want to understand their companies' profit and loss statements and balance sheeets. The SEC expects that by 1981 all oil and gas companies will report income, assets and liabilities on the basis of RRA. In the interim, the commission will allow slimmed-down versions of either full-cost or successful-efforts.

Here is what the RRA proposal says:

The business of an oil company is to find and produce reserves. So its financial results should be based on the *value*, *today*, of the reserves it discovers and produces. Full-cost and successful-efforts, by contrast, are both based upon classifying the *historical costs* of finding and producing reserves, on whether you consider those costs assets or expenses.

Take a simple example. Suppose you spend $100,000 on each of two fields. One field has oil—100,000 barrels of it. The other field is dry. Under successful-efforts, a company charges against income immediately the $100,000 exploration cost of the dry field and capitalizes the $100,000 cost of the producer. A dry hole cannot be an asset, it says in effect. The company using full-cost accounting capitalizes the entire $200,000 exploration cost. Theory: To be successful you must also be unsuccessful. Expense for this company: zero.

In neither case does the firm's balance sheet or P&L statement reflect oil discovered. This is relegated to footnote disclosure—sometimes.

Now RRA. It says the oil is worth $10 a barrel, so an asset worth $1 million was created. It took $200,000 to create the asset, so the net value is $800,000. That shows as an increase to stockholders' equity—and it is reflected on the income statement: "Income From Oil: $800,000."

"This is a current value concept in accounting for profits." says PMM's Graese. "Usually you do not recognize changes in the value of inventory in income statements until you sell that inventory. But under RRA you recognize value changes constantly." In other words, a company could simply sit on its reserves. If the value of the reserves doubles in five years, the company's reported profit also doubles—even if not a barrel of oil actually has been sold.

RRA will have a huge effect on any U.S. oil company with substantial reserves. FORBES asked Barry Good, Wall Street investment banker Morgan Stanley's highly regarded oil stock analyst, to discuss the RRA proposal's impact. Good had already worked up two examples; Standard Oil of Ohio and Atlantic Richfield Co., both big Prudhoe Bay, Alaska winners. Here's how Good figures the effect:

Last year Arco reported net producing properties valued at $2.6 billion. Using current-value estimates by J. S. Herold Associates of Greenwich, Conn., Good figures that RRA will force Arco to carry those same properties at—*$11.8 billion*. The effect is even greater for Sohio: Its net producing properties last year were carried at $1.7 billion. "Using the SEC method, the value would be $10.7 billion," says Good, adding that RRA may radically alter investors' perceptions of oil company debt ratios.

As an *idea*, as an accounting *principle*, the SEC's RRA method makes sense. If oil firms' shareholders' primary asset is reserves, why *not* disclose those reserves to stockholders? But as a practical matter RRA is probably just going to confuse the investors. Worse, it opens wide the door to unethical managements bent on hyping their stocks by manipulating their earnings.

The problem is this: Present-valuing reserves is more black art than science. Explains Price Waterhouse's Connor: "First you have to estimate reserves. Then you estimate production costs. Then you estimate a time period over which a reserve is depleted. Then estimate the current selling price. Then you must re-evaluate all those estimates constantly. That's a great deal of judgment!"

For example; Assume you have a field with five barrels in reserve. Today the value is $10 per barrel. If you produced those barrels immediately, you'd report, under RRA, reserve assets of $50. What if you produce and sell them over the next five years, at one barrel each year? What's the value for 1978 financial statements of a barrel to be sold in 1979? To answer that, management and the accountants must assume a discount rate. By decree the SEC makes *that* much easy: The discount shall be 10 percent annually. So one barrel sold next year at today's $10 price is worth today $9.09. A barrel produced in 1980 is *today* worth $8.26, and so on. By similar discounting at 10 percent a year over five years, the entire five-barrel reserve is presently worth $37.90. Again, that *assumes* one barrel produced and sold each year.

So far, so good. But, what if management changes its mind? What if it decides next year to produce the entire field? In that case the present value of the oil is $45.45, not $37.90. The company's earnings would suddenly jump by the difference, or $7.55. Nice maneuver.

Now let's look at that SEC-decreed uniform discount rate of 10 percent. Finance experts agree an asset's discount rate should reflect the risk of recovering the asset. If Peru, say, is on the verge of civil war, shouldn't reserves there be discounted more than reserves in Wyoming? Yes—but under the RRA proposal both reserves are discounted at 10 percent annually. Wyoming = Peru.

As we said, most accountants favor the *idea* of RRA. What scares them is the inherent imprecision of estimating and valuing reserves. The accountants say the SEC went too far. They want the reserve information that was disclosed in the footnotes, not reflected in the P&L and balance sheet. What's the difference? Answers PMM's Graese: "Once you crank this very soft information into the primary financial statements, you lend it an aura of precision that simply is not warranted."

Isn't there another troublesome question here? What about the SEC's often proclaimed support of the FASB as final accounting standards arbiter? Now that the SEC has overruled FASB Opinion 19, what becomes of the FASB?

At the moment no one knows. FASB Chairman Donald Kirk spoke to oil industry lawyers, accountants and analysts last month. Some members of the audience portrayed him as emotionless and careful to avoid controversy. An FASB staffer reports that the Board is now in the throes of deciding what it should, or can, do with Opinion 19.

For his part, SEC Chairman Williams, in announcing that his agency was overruling the FASB, reaffirmed the SEC's support for the beleaguered body.

Says Peat Marwick Mitchell's Graese, shaking his head: "I think it's pretty ironic that the SEC charged the FASB with settling on a single accounting method and then, after the FASB did that, turned around and allowed both [full-cost and successful-efforts] methods to be used."

The CPAs face still another worrisome prospect: all the irate stockholders and malpractice suits that will surely result from the freewheeling art of estimating and valuing reserves.

"Luckily we have Statement on Auditing Standards Number II," says Laventhol & Horwath partner Charles Chazen, "which sets forth our rights in hiring and using specialists, petroleum engineers in this case." But whether judges and juries will uphold these "rights"—which is to say, shift liability from CPAs to engineers—is anybody's guess.

It is not clear that the SEC's RRA will ever come to pass. "You know." says DLJ's Chalsty, "the SEC is putting together an advisory committee to help them get this thing going. My guess is that that committee will point out all the difficulties and perhaps convince the commission that RRA is impractical."

Maybe the SEC cannot legislate good accounting principles, as PMM's Graese says, but obviously it *can* legislate high incomes for special individuals. What is readily apparent is that the SEC has made the nation's petroleum engineers into hot commodities. "Oh yes," laughs SEC staffer James Russell, "they'll have their hands *and* their pockets full." ∎

October 2, 1978

4

ACCOUNTING
FOR INFLATION

We would guesstimate that maybe 50 percent of today's most glaring accounting problems are caused by one fact of modern life: persistent inflation at relatively high levels. In other words, if there were no (or even very low) inflation, then there would be far fewer critics of accounting principles than there are today. After all, what at heart is goodwill *and negative goodwill* but a difference between old values and new values? In the section following this one we explore the peculiar financial results caused when management prematurely retires discounted debt (see pages 101-118). But why is the debt discounted in the first place? Answer: inflation. Again, differences between national inflation rates are partly why nations' currencies rise and fall against one another; this foreign exchange rate volatility has helped make FASB Statement No. 8 probably the most controversial accounting rule since the Board's conception (see the readings beginning on page 119).

Solve inflation, and you eliminate lots of your critics. And if you can't whip inflation? At least accountants should be able to develop methods to *account* for it. In fact, you might wonder why, if inflation has been a serious problems for the last two or three decades—why the accountants have yet to agree on how to account for inflation's impact on balance sheets and income statements. Why the delay? What gives? It is this: There is no easy, logical, consistent way to adjust financial statements for the impact of inflation.

Do you think it's simply a matter of adjusting companies' financial data by changes in the general price level—if all prices rise 10 percent this year then cut U.S. Steel's nominal profits by 10 percent? If you think this is the answer read "Oops! We overlooked that!" (page 87), which shows how highly leveraged capital intensive public utilities would have *increased* substantially their reported earnings had the FASB implemented its Exposure Draft, "Financial Reporting in Units of General Purchasing Power" (which it didn't).

Perhaps you feel replacement cost accounting—the concept the SEC has been pushing, most recently on the oil and gas producers (see page 70 ff above)—is the way to go? Then read the epilogue to this section, in which MAPCO Chairman Robert E. Thomas uses some very strong language to blast replacement cost accounting.

There is this, too: What will be the government's attitude to inflation accounting? Suppose inflation-adjusted corporate profits are shown to be worth half their nominal levels. Will the government levy corporate income taxes at the prevailing tax rates against these much lower profits and therby forgo considerable revenues?

The sad fact is that the impact of inflation on financial statements is rather like cancer: Everyone agrees we *need* a cure but no one seems able to *find* a cure.

The accountants grapple with inflation

"It doesn't make any sense," they complain. "Our earnings are up 55 percent on a sales gain of 20 percent. Our backlogs have never been higher. And yet our stock dropped another four points last week. *You* explain it."

We hear that sort of thing from just about every company president we talk to these days.

So we trot out the usual answers: The energy crisis. Watergate. The individual investor's utter lack of interest in the market.

But is there a more fundamental reason why investors aren't impressed by all these hefty earnings gains? Could it be that they suspect those earnings gains are more apparent than real—because of inflation?

After all, companies that carry their inventories on first-in-first-out, matching oldest costs against latest prices, often report a lot of "profit" that comes simply from price rises that took place while they were in the warehouse. A few months ago the Treasury Department's chief economist, Dr. Herman Liebling, told us that "a little over half" of the gain in corporate profits in the first half of 1973 was of this illusory type.

And that's only one inflationary distortion. Then there are those straight-line depreciation charges for plants and refineries built 20 years ago. They're way too low because the purchasing power of those dollars has declined markedly in the interim. So you could make a strong case that such companies are running down capital and inflating earnings at the same time.

The situation is even worse with natural resource companies. Their most valuable assets aren't even *shown* on the balance sheet—all that oil that's still underground, all that unmined copper, all those vast tracts of uncut timber. If they were shown, return on assets would be a fraction of what it is today.

81

You can't blame managements for such distortions, of course. They didn't create inflation. And they have no choice but to follow generally accepted accounting principles in reporting their earnings. It's the accounting profession that ought to be doing something about it.

Well, to our pleasant surprise, the accountants *are*.

We mentioned, a few issues back, that Sandy Burton, the chief accountant of the Securities & Exchange Commission, is something of an activist. On January 3, the SEC strongly urged companies to disclose the amount of "inventory profits" included in their earnings. But that was just a first step, said the SEC. Perhaps "a fundamental change" in accounting methods might be necessary if inflation continues at its present unpleasant pace.

The accountants quickly took the hint. Two weeks later, after commenting tartly on the "creative tension" that exists between the profession's rule-making body and the SEC, Marshall Armstrong, chairman of the Financial Accounting Standards Board, announced that the FASB was looking into the matter and planned to come out with a pronouncement, perhaps as soon as midyear.

Specifically, Armstrong said the FASB was thinking of requiring companies to publish "supplemental price-level-adjusted" information beside each number on their balance sheets and income statements.

How would this adjustment work? What could investors learn from the adjusted numbers? Might this be only the first step toward even more fundamental changes in accounting?

To find out we talked to some senior men in the major accounting firms. The easiest way to measure inflation, they said, is to use one of the national price indices: the consumer price index, or the wholesale price index, for example. Each year, in order to figure out how much of the economy's growth is inflation and how much actual growth, the Government combines all of its indices into one percentage figure called the "gross national product deflator." Since the GNP deflator is the broadest-based price index, it is generally used to measure the extent to which the purchasing power of the dollar has declined due to inflation.

Now under price-level adjustment, the accountants continued, we would be applying the GNP deflator to all the dollar figures on corporate financial statements. Suppose, for example, the GNP deflator showed that we had had 10 percent inflation last year. And suppose that your company showed earnings of $12 million in 1972 and $15 million in 1973. If we applied price-level adjustment to that earnings figure, we'd see that company's "real" earnings growth was from $13.5 million in 1972 to $15 million in 1973. Measured in dollars of the same purchasing power, the earnings growth turns out to be less dramatic, you see.

Now go a step further, the accountants went on. Suppose the company is using straight-line depreciation, spreading the cost of its plant and equipment out over its expected life in equal amounts of, say, $20 million a year. If 1973 dollars have 10 percent less purchasing power than the 1972 dollars did, price-level adjustments for 1973 would raise the company's depreciation charges 10 percent to $22 million, which, of course, would further reduce its earnings. And on the asset side of the balance sheet, the adjustment would increase the 1973 undepreciated cost of its plant and equipment 10 percent.

Notice, the accountants warned, that we're *not* revaluing those assets or stating them at their present worth, we're simply translating that existing cost figure into its equivalent in present dollars.

What the FASB would probably do initially, the accountants figured, would be to require companies to show "adjusted" figures alongside the usual numbers for disclosure purposes only. A good many other countries have considered this approach also, most recently Great Britain. The computations were tricky, however, so the FASB might give U.S. companies until 1976 to get used to them before making such disclosure mandatory. After five years or so on a supplemental basis, the FASB might then take the far more controversial step of requiring companies to use adjusted figures internally and report only "adjusted" figures to shareholders. The taxing authorities might even adapt the adjustment for taxing purposes as well.

But wouldn't price-level adjustment hurt companies with a lot of fixed assets far more than other companies? we wondered. We put the question to Frank T. Weston, a senior partner of Arthur Young & Co. and a former member of the Accounting Principles Board.

"Yes," he replied. "But I don't think this is unfair, just realistic. After all, capital-intensive companies are helped more *now* on their income statements than other companies because of the fact that we don't now show depreciation on a price-level-adjusted basis."

What about the investor? we asked. What can he learn from these adjustments, say, in comparing two chemical companies?

"He could better judge how well different managements were reacting to inflation by increasing their debt, for example, which of course helps you during inflation, or by holding down the amount of capital tied up in receivables," Weston replied.

"As a matter of fact, the Board conducted an 18-company experiment with price-level adjustment back in 1969," he went on. "The companies made us promise we would never reveal their names because they knew, of course, that such adjustments would reduce their earnings. Well, you know, they were quite amazed at the results! Particularly the extent to which they would be helped by debt leverage."

But wait a minute now, we said. The Penn Central, like most railroads, was heavily leveraged. If Penn Central annual reports had contained price-level-adjusted figures prior to the collapse, would that have made any difference?

"They were charging you a ticket to ride based on 1952 costs," answered

Weston. "And you were paying in 1973 dollars. They were depreciating old equipment at old dollars and not raising revenues enough to keep purchasing power within the company because of regulation and the impact of trucking and the national highway system. With price-level adjustment, the regulatory bodies might have recognized this sooner."

Over at the Manhattan headquarters of Price Waterhouse in the newly security-conscious Exxon building, Henry Hill, PW's national director of accounting and auditing services, and PW senior partner Robert Hampton, another former member of the Accounting Principles Board, cautioned against expecting too much from price-level adjustment.

"Price-level adjustment very properly and vividly sets forth information that can be useful, provided people understand its imperfections and what it's trying to do." said Hill. "The adjustments do *not* show a company as if it hadn't had inflation. Inflation is too pervasive. And the adjustments are imperfect because you have to use some type of price index, which inevitably understates the actual impact of inflation on some companies and overstates it for others."

We thought about that for a moment. Price-level adjustment only measured the impact of inflation on dollars, not the impact of inflation on specific corporate assets and liabilities. And price-level adjustment still would not show the present worth of corporate assets. And the reserves of natural resource companies would still be missing from their balance sheets. Was there any way to eliminate those distortions?

Yes, answered the accountants. You could attempt some version of "current-value accounting."

How would *that* work we asked. We looked out the office window at the skyscraper-studded Manhattan skyline. How on earth could a company determine the present worth of the new corporate headquarters it built five years ago and planned to use for the next 20 or 30 years?

Frank Weston picked that one up. He's a longtime advocate of current-value accounting. "Well, first you decide whether the chief value to the company of that building is its future rental and resale value, or its utility value in place," he explained. "If it's the former, as it would be for a real estate company, you value it based on its estimated life and estimated future lease revenues—figuring in probable inflation and future taxes. If it's the latter, as would be the case for the manufacturing facilities of most industrial companies, you use something called 'replacement cost,' which is the cost in present dollars to build facilities using today's technology having a comparable productive capacity."

Whoa! we protested. Not so fast! How does "replacement cost" as you describe it tell us the present worth of a steel mill built in 1952?

"O.K.," answered Weston. "This is a compromise solution. Let's say your steel mill ships 1 million tons of steel a year. In order to arrive at the replacement cost or current value of that property charged against your present production, we would have to visualize a new steel mill that also turns out 1 million tons of steel, but one that was built today, reflecting today's efficiencies and prices.

"This approach is not necessarily more difficult than present methods," Weston added. "Companies do a lot of this type of cost analysis today that doesn't get on the books, you know."

Across town, at Price Waterhouse, Robert Hampton and Henry Hill shook their heads. An academic proposal. "Frankly, I don't have that much faith in the estimation process for the determination of current values," said Hampton. "The practical difficulty, of course, is who is going to do the measuring—the guessing of what that current value is."

Academic? Not really. For some time Dutch companies have been permitted to use the "replacement cost" concept on their financial statements. Today an estimated 15 percent of them do so—including big Philips Lamp, which keeps both inventories and fixed assets on replacement cost. And what would Philips' net income have looked like if it used U.S. generally accepted accounting principles? Well, according to its most recent annual report, 1972 net income would have been higher to the tune of $48.3 million! Quite a difference, even for a company with earnings in U.S. dollars (and U.S. accounting principles) of nearly $257 million.

We told Frank Weston what Hill and Hampton were saying about his current value arguments.

"Well, I'd reply this way." he said with a smile. "If we can get people all computing depreciation on replacement cost, then we've taken out of the income statement the differences due to the fact that one company built their plant in 1952 and another company in the same industry built a plant just like it in 1960 with cheaper dollars."

In other words, the guy who built his plant in 1952 has artificially higher earnings because his depreciation charges are lower? we asked.

"Exactly," Weston replied. "Now if they were both on replacement cost you could better see the true differences between the companies."

But, clearly, the greatest advantage of all for current-value accounting, Weston concluded, would be that at last a dollar value would be placed on all those underground oil and mineral reserves of the extractive industries. And a much fairer picture of the present worth of real estate developers would emerge.

"Supplemental price-level-adjusted figures are a worthwhile move that could be taken in the near future," said Weston. "Changes to current value would take longer. We'll just have to take one step at a time and see what the impact of all these changes looks like as we go along."

Are you confused by inflation accounting? Well, you ought to be. Even the accountants seem to have difficulty sorting out the fine points. And their corporate clients, of course, are stoutly opposed to *all* of it. It's you, the user of financial statements, the individual or institutional investor, whom the accountants are doing this for. And we came away from these conversations feeling that the effort was well worth it.   ∎

March 1, 1974

B

Oops!
We overlooked that

What worries us about the accountants is the profession's occasional tendency to make things worse in a sincere but confused effort to make them better. The latest case in point is the Financial Accounting Standards Board's exposure draft on inflation accounting, which is now being circulated through the profession and through industry generally.

The proposal is, in essence, to apply a single general-purchasing-power adjustment to all figures of all companies—and report the figures so adjusted as a supplement to their regular financial statements. Unfortunately, the FASB exposure draft also has a grave flaw—one that FASB members themselves admit they completely overlooked.

What is behind the proposal, of course, is the havoc that inflation has played with figures based on historical cost: Assets depreciated or depleted on the basis of their historical cost cannot be replaced by the total of the amounts thus reserved. What the FASB proposed is to adjust such historically based figures by a general, nationwide index of inflation—the gross national product deflator, for example.

This is a crude adjustment at best, since inflation rates vary from industry to industry and from one geographical area to the next. Thus, while the adjusted figures may come closer to current realities, it is almost coincidental whether they reflect accurately the fair market value of an item or its cost of replacement.

You would expect that any kind of inflation adjustment would tend to reduce reported earnings because it would increase depreciation charges every year in line with the inflation rate. A company with $10 million in depreciation, given a 10 percent inflation rate, would have to reserve $11 million the next year even if it didn't buy a single new machine. So, pretax earnings "drop" by $1 million.

But that is only half the story. You have to consider the effect of inflation on liabilities as well as on assets. Inflation reduces *liabilities* in terms of real dollars; when you pay off the debt, you do so in cheaper dollars. Under this new kind of accounting, a company loses earnings from higher depreciation but gains earnings from the reduction of the debt. The exposure draft provides that this gain on debt be credited directly to earnings.

Please follow us in some simple arithmetic. A company borrows $100 at the start of 1974 and buys a machine with it. By the beginning of 1975, after a year of 12 percent inflation, the company is permitted to take a $12 credit because the debt has decreased by that amount in constant dollars. But now let's look at the machine. It gets written up to $112—although the extra $12 isn't flowed through to income—with the result that depreciation charges go up. Let's take 10 percent straight-line depreciation. Under present rules the depreciation is $10; under the new rules it is $11.20—10 percent of $112.

The bottom line now looks like this. Credit to earnings: $12. Debit to earnings from higher depreciation: $1.20. Net gain: $10.80. Terrific!

But wait a minute. We're sorry to say that there's yet another complication. Any business has receivables: cash due it. Obviously, these receivables are depreciating in value during a period of inflation. Like debt, these are "monetary" items. So, while the company gets a *credit* for the reduction in the burden of its debt, it gets *debited* for the reduction of its receivables.

This is rough on a company with high receivables and little debt. Such a company gets hit by inflation accounting on *both* sides of the balance sheet. Take Eastman Kodak, which last year had about $1.6 billion in receivables and cash items and $1.2 billion in debt. On 12 percent inflation, Kodak would gain a credit of about $144 million on its debt, but would "lose" $192 million on its receivables. Moreover, its depreciation charges would rise by more than $25 million. Overall, Kodak's earnings would have been lowered by $73 million. This, of course, oversimplifies the situation, but makes the point that a conservatively financed company would be penalized under the proposed rules.

Restated this way, most companies earnings *do* come out lower than those they reported. In a recent book, *Accounting—The Language of Business,* Professor Sidney Davidson of the University of Chicago Business School and three colleagues applied the FASB guidelines to the 1974 results of 65 industrial companies. The 30 Dow Jones industrial companies showed a median reduction in earnings to 88 percent of reported earnings. For the other 35 companies, the median was 94 percent. Some companies were tremendously impacted. Chrysler, for example, would have shown triple the loss it reported. General Motors would have shown a loss, and United Technologies' restated earnings would have been only 25 percent of those actually reported in 1974.

Still others would have been little affected, and some would have benefited. Procter & Gamble's restated earnings would have been 98 percent of the $317 million it did report. Alcoa, more highly leveraged, would have shown 27 percent greater earnings by restatement.

That set Davison to thinking. He decided to look at some highly leveraged industries. In an article to appear in the September-October issue of *The Financial Analysts Journal*, he and Roman Weil of Georgia Tech report on the consequences of applying the FASB guidelines to the utilities.

The results, if the pun is permissible, are electrifying. Utility earnings would have increased in every case, usually by more than double. The impact on earnings per share was even more dramatic. As shown in the table on page 90, median earnings per share of electric utilities would triple.

Are utility earnings so much better than anyone except possibly Ralph Nader suspected? Rather the opposite, in fact. If one elminated monetary item adjustments (*see column two of the table*), all the companies showed sharp earnings *declines*. Consumers Power, a Michigan utility generally considered in trouble, showed restated earnings only 37 percent of those reported. But include monetary items, and Consumers Power would show restated earnings more than triple and per-share earnings six times those that were reported.

Consumers Power shows this precisely *because* it is in such woeful shape. As a highly leveraged utility its "earnings" from discounted debt are huge, but without any more cash flow—it is all a paper profit. "It sounds as though a company could show huge earnings gains all the way to bankruptcy," snaps Controller Ralph Heumann of Chicago's Commonwealth Edison, echoing the fears of many other utilities.

It's not that the utilities are constitutionally opposed to inflation adjustments. Some, like Indiana Telephone and Toledo Edison, already publish inflation-adjusted figures. But both *defer* the benefit of inflation on long-term debt, and that has the effect of sharply *decreasing* earnings—not increasing them as would the FASB approach. Indiana Telephone, for example, has restated earnings of $1.93, *vs.* $3.96 on a historical cost basis—an approach that its auditors, Arthur Andersen & Co., say in their letter of certification *more fairly* represents the true financial condition of the company.

What worries the utilities is that rate-making commissions might treat the higher restated earnings as true current earnings—something that FASB Vice Chairman Robert Sprouse expressed a fervent hope would not occur. But rate commissions are more noted for their grasp of political expediency than their grasp of accounting intricacy.

The heart of the utility objection is the FASB's different treatment of monetary items, like debt and receivables, and nonmonetary items, like plant and equipment. They would prefer both items to be treated the same way in regulated industries, where the allowed return is based on recovery of historical cost. Sprouse concedes this problem, although it never came up in the FASB committee's initial discussions.

Electric Utilities Earnings, FASB Style

Utility	Reported 1974 income (millions)	—Adjusted Income— Before gain on monetary items (millions)	Including gain on monetary items (millions)	Common Share Earnings Reported	Adjusted
American Elec. Power	$176	$117	$488	$2.06	$7.21
Cleveland Elec. Illum.	61	45	127	3.68	9.60
Commonwealth Edison	180	108	395	2.88	8.21
Consolidated Edison	209	148	499	2.68	8.79
Consumers Power	61	23	202	1.34	8.31
Detroit Edison	89	55	255	1.46	6.00
Houston Lighting & Power	69	54	149	2.92	6.98
Niagara Mohawk Power	96	65	216	1.70	4.86
Pacific Gas & Elec.	261	179	515	3.27	8.24
Philadelphia Elec.	129	94	294	1.81	5.94
Public Service Elec. & Gas	154	106	351	2.35	7.03
Southern Calif. Edison	218	169	409	4.10	9.76

Source: Financial Analysts Journal, September/October, 1975.

What kind of inflation accounting will be used by U.S. business is not merely a question of adjusting the disagreement between the utilities and the FASB. The Securities & Exchange Commission is likely to enter the fray with its own preferred method, replacement-cost accounting, which restates fixed assets and inventory on the balance sheet and cost of sales and depreciation in the income statement in terms of replacement cost. It also raises the confusing prospect that financial statements could show *three* sets of numbers: the traditional, the FASB's and the SEC's, although the latter two sets of figures would be supplementary to the first.

Replacement-cost accounting is admittedly more complex than the FASB method, which John C. Burton, the SEC's chief accountant, argues is confusing and does not reflect financial reality. But one can agree with Burton's reservations without accepting the SEC's alternative.

It's too bad that life isn't simple, but since it is so complicated, the accountants and the regulatory authorities should work together rather than at cross purposes so that they don't end up confusing investors instead of better informing them. ∎

August 15, 1975

EPILOGUE: Late in 1975, under intense pressure from the SEC and the business community, the FASB withdrew its proposed rule calling for general-price-level-adjusted financial statements. The Board's technicians headed back to the drawing boards, from which they rebounded strongly in January 1979.

Inflation?
Account for it

It would drive entire British industries, like textiles, deeply into the red. British shipping profits would be wiped out. Industries like banking, construction and retailing would be hurt far less: Their earnings would only be trimmed from 10 percent to 30 percent. It would be sure to confuse many shareholders and a fair number of financial experts as well.

"It" is "current cost accounting," the most comprehensive and revolutionary approach to inflation accounting under serious consideration in the world today.

Despite the devastating effect it would have on British corporate earnings, the proposed new method is strongly favored by most U.K. businessmen. For example, the exhaustively detailed accounting standards were declared "sensible" and "realistic" by Jan Hildreth, director general of the Institute of Directors, when they were proposed by the Morpeth Steering Committee Group several weeks ago. And James Forbes, finance director of Cadbury Schweppes Ltd., the $1.1-billion-sales candy and beverage maker said, "I am confident that larger companies will adopt the new standards as quickly as possible."

Why the enthusiasm for something that would clobber earnings? Anthony Frodsham, director general of the Engineering Employers Federation, put his finger on the reason: "No industry can survive for long when the prices it charges for its products are in real terms only marginally profitable and when it is being taxed on profits that may not really exist."

The villain, of course, is Britain's runaway inflation, which is destroying the very foundation of its financial certainty. Indeed, one of the main complaints from English industrialists who have lived with one of the worst inflation rates in the industrialized world over five years now is that current cost accounting will not be imposed soon enough.

In the U.S. the possibility that inflation could soon be as uncontrollable as in Britain makes the Morpeth proposals of vital interest. Here is how current cost accounting would work on a British balance sheet:

- Corporate land and buildings would be valued by professional real estate experts at least once ,every five years (or more frequently if there were significant changes such as the addition of land or buildings). The new evaluations would determine the market value of the property as it was currently being used by the company. (In contrast, land and buildings are presently carried on both U.S. and British balance sheets at historical costs.) The bottom line of this revaluation would be to increase annual depreciation charges and thus reduce reported profits.

- Inventory and work in progress would be shown on the balance sheet at current replacement costs or net realizable value—whichever is lower. This would be roughly comparable to U.S. companies following last-in, first-out inventory accounting and would eliminate inventory profits of the kind that so overstated the earnings of U.S. companies during the hyperinflation of 1974.

- To show how inflation hurts the overall purchasing power of stockholders' equity, a separate statement would compare shareholders' worth at year's end (including any gains) to what it had been at the beginning of the year, multiplied by any percentage gain in the consumer price index. Simply, if stockholders' equity increased 15 percent over the year, but the consumer price index went up 25 percent in the same period, the new statement would show an overall 10 percent decline in the purchasing power of stockholders' equity.

Meantime, on the British profit and loss statement:

During periods of inflation, almost any revaluation of assets during the year would lower pretax profit by increasing depreciation charges based on current (higher) replacement costs. To show the stockholders how this increased depreciation charge would be used, an "appropriations account" would appear under the after tax net profit statement. In the new account, theoretically, such surplus would be added almost entirely to a revaluation reserve (or replacement cost reserve). But a company might withhold (or subtract) a substantial amount from this reserve, for example, when it decided to replace fixed assets using borrowed money. In that case, the withheld (or subtracted) portion would be added to after tax profit for dispersal through dividends, passed on to another, specific, reserve, or, with profits left over after dividends, added to the general reserve (retained earnings).

The appropriations account has aroused controversy. Astute analysts like

Martin Gibbs, senior research partner of London stockbrokers Phillios & Drew, are quick to point out the potential for manipulation, since management decides how much of the surplus can be used for dividends.

To which Christopher Westwick, technical director of the Morpeth committee, replies, "Whatever companies do, they've got to explain and justify it to the stockholders, and my idea of manipulation is something that goes on that people can't see."

What about taxes? Would the British equivalent of Internal Revenue accept the greatly reduced profit figures for tax purposes? There is a good chance that it would, since it has so little to lose. Only 3.5 percent of Britain's tax revenues come from corporate income taxes, *vs.* 14.6 percent in the U.S.

The closer current cost accounting comes to reality, the more specific become the objections and the complexities. Patrick J. Custis, director of finance of the $2-billion-sales steel, tool and machinery producer Guest Reed & Nettlefolds, asks this question: "To value an obsolescent asset for balance-sheet purposes may justify the use of an estimate of the value of its modern equivalent, but can the resulting charge for depreciation be regarded as representing the current cost of the existing asset?"

In plain English, Custis is saying that an old machine is an old machine, and it isn't reasonable to depreciate it as though it were a spanking new modern one. Custis' firm has a great deal of old machinery. Stockbroker Martin Gibbs estimates that GR&N's earnings, calculated conventionally, would drop 98 percent under current cost accounting.

There is a price

Is it worth it? Geoffrey Rowett, an accountant by training and managing director of Charterhouse Group, a $200-million-sales holding company, has his doubts: "What worries us is the complexity of trying rapidly to introduce technical accounting procedures and the difficulty of getting other countries geared up to them."

Still, most English businessmen would agree with Unilever's David Orr: "The price of delay is too damaging for industry to continue to bear."

There seems to be little question that some version of the Morpeth standards, however subsequently expanded, will take effect this year in the U.K. There seems equally little question that the U.S. is presently heading in the same direction—and the supplementary-replacement-cost disclosure now required by the SEC is but a modest first step. ■

March 1, 1977

Steel:
Biting the bullet

Bethlehem Steel is facing the fact that it's reported earnings have been grossly overstated. The rest of the U.S. steel industry has yet to do so.

Has U.S. Steel, like Bethlehem, been overstating its profits in recent years? Bracy Smith, U.S. Steel's vice president-comptroller, sadly concedes that it has.

This doesn't mean that U.S. Steel is preparing its stockholders for the kind of blow that Bessie's stockholders took last month when the number-two steel company reported a $750-million writeoff that exceeded by 50 percent its pretax earnings for the previous two full years. Bessie's writeoff was precipitated by the decision to close its vast but outdated Lackawanna, N.Y. mills. Though U.S. Steel is considering plant shutdowns, it hopes to avoid a closing on such a large scale.

But U.S. Steel—and the rest of the steel industry—shares with Bethlehem the kind of unrealistic bookkeeping that caused Bessie to take, in the third quarter of 1977, costs and expenses that it ought to have taken years ago. Close to $170 million of the writeoff involved the remaining book value of the plant operations being shut down—suggesting that Bessie's bookkeeping did not recognize reality so far as obsolescence was concerned.

Nor, it seems, does U.S. Steel's bookkeeping. The financial figures tell the tale. In 1967, on a gross property account of $8 billion and net sales of $4 billion, U.S. Steel took $357 million in depreciation and depletion charges. Last year, on $12 billion in plant and $8.6 billion in sales, it charged off only $309 million. In other words, depreciation fell from 4.5 percent on gross plant and 9 percent on sales to 2.5 percent on gross plant and under 4 percent on sales.

How realistic can those figures be in a period of inflation, when replacement costs are constantly climbing? The *Quality of Earnings Report* recently performed an interesting dissection on U.S. Steel's income statement.

In 1976, the report points out, U.S. Steel reported earnings of $5.03 a share, but had it used different bookkeeping it could have shown less than half that amount. The chief problem with Big Steel's accounting, the report says, was that it reported depreciation on a straight-line basis rather than on an accelerated basis. It also flowed through the investment credit immediately into income. But U.S. Steel used the more conservative depreciation method in reporting to Internal Revenue—to lessen the tax bite. In effect, U.S. Steel told its stockholders it had earned $5.03 but confided to IRS that a more realistic figure was substantially less.

Thornton O'glove, author of the report, is careful to point out the U.S. Steel is hardly unique among American corporations in this double-standard reporting. According to *Accounting Trends and Techniques*, a publication of the American Institute of Certified Public Accountants, a solid majority of U.S. companies use straight-line depreciation for shareholder reporting purposes. (A majority also use the flow-through method for the investment tax credit.) But since steel is so capital-intensive and since its technology has changed so drastically, the distortions of inflation on the profit-and-loss statement are especially dramatic for this industry.

FORBES asked U.S. Steel's vice president-comptroller whether the steel industry has been hurt by the fact that its profits were overstated. Interestingly, Bracy Smith didn't disagree. "I suspect that it has, because people say. 'Hell, You're making this much money; why do you need more?'" That's the attitude the industry faces when it tries to persuade the government that it needs price relief, or less rigid pollution-control requirements; it's also the attitude the industry faces at contract negotiating time with its unions.

So why does U.S. Steel compound the problem of overstated earnings by using straight-line depreciation and flowing through the investment tax credit? Smith's reply: We changed to those methods in 1968, but didn't want to. "We found ourselves in a position where everyone else in the industry, and industry generally, had departed from accelerated depreciation," Smith says. "We looked rather foolish, socking all that additional depreciation against our income, and being compared on a completely different basis."

Smith is right: Nearly every major steel company switched to straight-line depreciation at some point in 1968. The move was started by smaller companies like Armco, which feared that the slump in steel stocks that year would create an irresistible inducement for high-flying conglomerates to take them over. Jones & Laughlin Steel was snapped up by Ling-Temco-Vought; Crucible Steel merged with Colt Industries, and Lykes Corp. with Youngstown Sheet & Tube. Nervous steel managements decided to boost reported earnings—thereby hopefully boosting their stocks. In the third quarter, Armco, Inland, Republic, and several others changed to straight-line depreciation, and Inland got an extra shot of accounting profits by switching to the flow-through method for reporting the investment tax credit (which Armco and Republic had already adopted). The results were comforting–if falsely so. Third-quarter reported earnings were 35 percent higher for Republic than they would have been under the conservative method; for Armco the figure was 25 percent, for Inland 30 percent. The companies correctly pointed out that they were only following accounting practices already used by much of American industry.

The three biggest companies, U.S. Steel, Bethlehem, and National, were less concerned about being taken over, but they joined the switch later that year. In U.S. Steel's 1968 annual report, the company explained to its shareholders that it considered the more conservative practices of accelerated depreciation and deferred investment tax credit to be "preferable." But to "enhance the comparability" of its financial statements with others in the steel industry and U.S. business generally, the company would switch to the straight-line and flow-through methods. The two changes, the report continued, contributed $1.74 to 1968 earnings per share of $4.69–a nice boost to reported profit, but of course neither change added a penny to U.S. Steel's cash flow.

U.S. Steel's Bracy Smith argues that it was impossible for U.S. Steel to stand alone against the crowd unless it was willing to see its stock suffer. "We would be very happy if they would make the rule that everyone has to take accelerated depreciation on their books," he says. "That would begin to take some of the screwiness out of the figures. But you can't have just one company doing it." Lee Seidler, a New York University accounting professor and highly respected authority, sympathetically agrees that a company has to consider the effect of its accounting policies on its ability to raise money in the capital markets. But, he adds, "I would suppose that the fact that management holds stock options and things of that sort may sway their judgment."

Smith's point that it is difficult to stand alone in reporting lower profits may be correct, but the fact is that a number of large, successful companies use conservative depreciation and/or investment tax credit reporting methods. Among them: E.I. Du Pont, Dow Chemical, Caterpillar Tractor, McGraw-Edison, Johnson & Johnson, Corning Glass. In Du Pont's case, using accelerated depreciation and the deferred method for reporting the investment tax credit made the company's 1976 earnings of $459 million ($9.30 a share) appear about $150 million ($3.10 a share) lower than they would have been under more generous accounting methods. Apparently Du Pont, Dow and the others believe that there is some truth to the "efficient market hypothesis" of accounting–which says that the stock market will award a premium to high-quality earnings, and will take puffed-up earnings with a grain of salt. In the meantime, these companies can deal more realistically with unions, government regulators and the like when it comes time to discussing their industries' needs.

If you factor in inflation, the steel industry's position is even worse than it appears in Thornton O'glove's figures. Professor Seidler has carefully studied the steel industry for the Wall Street house of Bear, Stearns & Co. Had the steel industry depreciated its plant on a replacement cost basis rather than on historical cost, Seidler says, some of the companies would have been in the red during recent years. For example, in 1973 U.S. Steel reported earnings of $367 million (after taxes actually paid to the government). But on replacement cost accounting, he says, it would instead have *lost* $374 million. In short, in that year U.S. Steel's depreciation charges fell $750 million short of reality. U.S. Steel, in brief, has been living off its capital. So has the entire steel industry and many other capital-intensive industries.

Bethlehem Steel has started to bite the bullet. The rest of the U.S. steel industry has yet to do so. ■

December 1, 1972

EPILOGUE: In March 1976, the SEC issued "Accounting Series Release No. 190" which required approximately 1,000 of the largest publicly-owned U.S. manufacturing corporations to begin accounting for the value of their assets and liabilities on a replacement cost basis, disclosing the results in the 10-K Report filed annually with the SEC, and referring to this information in the footnotes to the financial statements. (For the time being the balance sheet and income statements themselves continue to be determined under historical cost.) The companies have gone along with the SEC's mandate—not that they have much choice, and certainly not without considerable bitter grumbling. Some of the loudest public griping came from MAPCO Inc. Chairman, Robert E. Thomas, who spoke for many an executive when he devoted an entire page of MAPCO's 1976 annual report to blasting replacement cost accounting:

For the first time, this Annual Report refers to accounting information dealing with "replacement cost accounting" which purports to show that inflation is really consuming a portion of MAPCO's profits as reported on a historical conventional accounting basis. The purported conclusions represent only a portion of the story—and because only a portion of the story is set forth, presents a misleading, highly distorted picture. In short, the conclusions are hogwash.

To begin with, replacement cost accounting assumes all assets being replaced currently at present prices with a resulting higher depreciation expense and thus lower profits. The government accountants at the Securities and Exchange Commission responsible for dreaming up this statistical aberration have completely ignored one simple fact of life—that if all industry were to replace all assets at today's costs, sales prices would be correspondingly higher . . .

. . . It is truly expensive hogwash and can be of benefit only to the revenues of U.S. appraisal and valuation firms.

Strong language, that. But the SEC has made no signs that it will abandon current value accounting, one form of which is replacement cost accounting. In fact, the Commission seems set on *expanding* its use: reserve recognition accounting, mandated by the SEC for the oil and gas producers (See page 72 above) is another form of current value accounting.

Has the FASB dropped the inflation-accounting ball altogether? Not at all. In early 1979, the FASB called a press conference to issue Exposure Drafts "Financial Reporting and Changing Prices" and "Constant Dollar Accounting." The final pronouncement, Statement of Financial Accounting Standards No. 33 was issued in late September 1979. The statement comes down on both sides of the issue and requires companies that are subject to the SFAS to report on both a current cost and a constant dollar basis. The 127-page statement is extremely complex and has been depicted by one Board member as "experimental."

5 LIABILITIES

Thus far, *Forbes Numbers Game* selections have dealt primarily with classifying and valuing assets. But with assets, so with liabilities: they are not always, maybe not even usually, what they seem to be. We think you'll agree with that assessment after reading the pieces that comprise this section.

What are the problems with liabilities? To start with a basic problem, you can never be sure, from merely looking at a balance sheet, that all material liabilities have been disclosed. The most troubling example of this arises in the reporting (should we say: non-reporting?) of pension fund liabilities. The article "Phantom pensions" (page 107) shows in ghastly detail how New York and other cities have consistently buried their unfunded pension obligations. But *corporate* investors had better take note too: The problem may be as widespread among companies as cities. (We cannot help but wonder if there is a connection here between unfunded and undisclosed pension fund liabilities on the one hand, and a severely depressed stock market on the other. Does "the market" know more about unfunded pension obligations than the balance sheets tell?)

Then there is the problem of classifying liabilities. Even when an obligation is on the balance sheet, is it in the right place? Our first reading in this section, "All debts are not equal," points out that, until recently anyway, all too many current liabilities were masquerading as long-term debt. One rather frightening implication of this: the accounting rules—GAAP—themselves may have been responsible for trapping some unwary, unsophisticated investors in the Penn Central bankruptcy debacle. Obviously, proper classification of liabilities is not to be taken lightly.

And finally we have the intriguing case of how some clever businessmen boost their reported profits by manipulating their liabilities (see "Now you see it . . ." page 110, and "Paper money," page 114). Here the issue is retiring discounted debt before it matures and taking the discount into earnings. Its a cute little gimmick that remains very much in vogue, as the epilogue notes.

All debts
are not equal

As the Greek philosopher Epictetus once said, some things in this world are not and yet appear to be.

Take debt. "It used to be easy," says Robert May, a partner at Arthur Anderson & Co. "There was no question a 25-year bond would mature in 25 years, and that it went under long-term debt on the balance sheet. And a 60-day bank loan or a 90-day note or piece of commercial paper would go under current liabilities."

Not any more. For new plant and equipment, say, a company may sell commercial paper in the short-term market through a dealer like Goldman Sachs or Salomon Bros.–intending eventually to refinance long term. Or it may obtain a five-year bank loan but, because the bank prefers it that way, handle the actual financing with 90-day notes, which it must keep turning over. So what is it? Long-term debt? Or current liabilities?

The accounting profession is trying to decide whether to do something about this debt illusion. "We are trying to get the real story, even if a company *says* it has its long-term financing tied up with a pretty yellow ribbon," says George R. Vogt, a partner at Peat Marwick Mitchell & Co. Haunting the auditors is the ghost, Penn Central. Penn Central was deep into bank debt and commercial paper, but calling it long-term debt. Why? Because the railroad felt it had commitments by lenders to keep rolling over the short-term stuff. Suddenly those commitments disappeared, and it was good-bye Pennsy.

If the auditors had been armed with a new accounting standard expected to go into effect January 1, they might have blown the whistle on Penn Central. The rule, as proposed by the Financial Accounting Standards Board, would require that commercial paper and other short-term financing (one year and less) be very clearly labeled: current liabilites. (Exception: a) the borrower has a "non-cancelable binding agreement" to refinance the debt from a financially able source; b) the debt will mature over a year from the date of the balance sheet; and c) the borrower intends to carry out the refinancing.)

So *what*, you may ask? What do I care whether it's called long-term debt or short-term debt so long as the company is solvent? Answer: You'd better care. The new rules make it tougher for companies to borrow money.

And look who's vulnerable! None other than American Telephone & Telegraph, that most creditworthy of our giant corporations. Ma Bell, which is usually on the side of the angels when it comes to tightening up accounting standards, is fighting mad against this one. Warren W. Brown, an assistant controller at AT&T, is the man who watches these things for the company, and so we asked him to explain. "The new rule," he told FORBES, "would make us pull the $1.7 billion that we now call the interim debt along with the $60 million in long-term debt that would have to be refinanced this year, and move it all down into current liabilities. Now that is an improper presentation."

Brown explains that AT&T thinks that the heading "current liabilities" ought to reflect cash needed for current operations—not debt that AT&T can easily refinance.

"Disappearing" Debt

One seeming improvement, of course, would be to lower AT&T's debt ratio from 47.6 percent to 46 percent. But where the change would really hurt AT&T is in its rate hearings. As *current liabilities*, the money would not count in its capital base in figuring the company's permissible rate of return. AT&T argues that this is dead wrong, because most of the money has already been put into plant and equipment under construction.

"The regulators," Brown went on, "use what is called telephone plant for our rate base. They figure this on total average capital, which consists of equity capital, long-term debt, interim debt and that long-term debt due to expire, but which is going to be refinanced." They do not consider current liabilities as capital.

Brown argues that AT&T has already gone a long way toward meeting the accountants' worries. Last year the company reached a compromise with the Securities & Exchange Commission when it agreed to set up "interim debt" as a separate category from long-term debt. But calling it interim debt is one thing, calling it short-term liabilities is something else again.

AT&T's interim debt on last September 30 consisted of $955 million in short-term bank loans and $925 million in commercial paper. Its outstanding commercial paper has more than doubled this year because of its huge construction budget and the sick state of the long-term capital market. The commercial paper has been backed, in effect, by $1 billion that AT&T carries under current assets as cash and temporary investments. But the temporary investments are advances in individual Bell System units to maintain their debt-to-net-worth ratios when they go to the debt market.

Granted, the accountants have provided for exceptions. But to take advantage of the exceptions, AT&T would need binding contracts from lenders to refinance their short-term loans. Could the lenders provide such contracts? "In my opinion," says controller Brown, "we could not get non-cancelable binding agreements. How in the world could we have binding agreements with the hundreds of banks around the country from whom we take short-term borrowings and do refinancing?"

As a bank officer in a leading New York City bank points out, lenders usually agree to refinance as long as there is no "material adverse change" in a company's position by the financing date. The ambiguity is purposeful, and protects banks against further Penn Centrals. "This is a critical point, though," says Arthur Andersen's May. "One adverse change might be that a company can't sell its paper. That gives us a lot of concern."

In AT&T's view, the proposed rule change might throw off some of the utility's critical ratios without really giving the average investor any better understanding of the company.

"The purpose of our balance sheet is not to inform an investor so much as it is to inform a creditor," says Brown. "The creditor is interested in your current ratio. We don't think that sophisticated users of our statement are misled by the presentation of debt we're now following."

"Today's financial statements are not prepared only for the sophisticated," counters George Vogt of Peat Marwick. "Every investor needs to understand a company's liquidity position."

While the rule change could prove annoying for AT&T, it would cut even deeper for the other telephone companies like General Telephone & Electronics and Continental Telephone. Continental now carries its commercial paper in short-term debt and interim categories, like AT&T. GT&E keeps around $570 million of its commercial paper outstanding, plus $323 million in short-term bank loans, *out* of current liabilities by listing it under a category called "short-term obligations."

The real blow, however, might be to utilities like Boston Edison, whose credit rating has been dropped on three different occasions in the past few years by Moody's. Once AAA, it's now down to Baa. Faced with tough going in the public market, Boston Edison has doubled its short-term borrowings from its 1973 average to over $145 million in August. Not included in the short-term load, but carried as long-term debt, is $60 million in short-term notes.

Once auditors start out to pin down and disclose financing agreements, there's no telling where the trail will lead. What about the $4.9 billion in commercial paper that the General Motors Acceptance Corp. has outstanding? Is *that* a current liability? What about Chrysler Corp.'s $1.4 billion in unsecured short-term notes?

Brown of AT&T argues that the rule should be limited to companies with lower credit ratings, which should be watched for signs of insolvency. "That's where the danger lies," he says. The SEC, however, is urging the accountants on. John (Sandy) Burton, chief SEC accountant, says firmly: "I don't see why one class of company, or companies with certain ratings, should get off the hook. It ought to apply across the board."

"We are going to be taking a lot closer look at those credit agreements from now on," says accountant May. While it's hard to say who's right, it is comforting to know that the accountants are finally trying to lock the barn doors through which so many purloined horses have passed. ∎

December 15, 1974

Phantom pensions?

No matter how New York City manages to survive its current billion-dollar budget bind, it will soon have to face an even more ominous time bomb—the city's employee pension system.

There is a tendency to blame the city's fiscal mess on welfare costs. Partially true: Unlike most localities, which pay little toward welfare, New York City assumes about 20 percent of its welfare burden. But many of the city employees who scream about welfare abuses have proved equally adept at exploiting the city's taxpayers. City expenditures for employee pensions and Social Security amounted to $1.1 billion in fiscal 1973-74, virtually equal to welfare costs of $1.2 billion.

New York City's pensions are the most generous overall of any large municipality in the nation. Almost all city employees—whether policemen or garbage collectors, foremen or subway workers—can now retire at half pay or more after only 20 or 25 years on the job. If a worker stays longer, his pension benefits go still higher. A 55-year-old teacher with 30 years' service can retire at two-thirds of his final salary. No private business could afford such pension costs. But then, businessmen don't have to run for reelection.

Years ago, comparatively liberal benefits made up for low salaries. But no more. City salaries are now 25 percent to 30 percent higher than those in private industry. Thus a *typical* New York cop can earn $20,000 a year pounding the beat and get $10,000 a year after he hangs up his nightstick. Okay, the policeman risks his life, but the average garbageman gets about $15,000 and can retire as early as age 40 on $7,500 a year.

These lush pension benefits come on top of federal Social Security benefits. They also come on top of annuity funds, financed almost entirely by the city's taxpayers, which give workers thousands of extra dollars upon retirement. Some teachers, for example, can walk away with a lump sum of $10,000 after 20 years.

The city's openhandedness knows no bounds. Except for those hired after mid-1973, the city determines a worker's pension not on the basis of his average salary for the last three or five years, but on his final year's salary or even on his last day's pay rate. Result: City employees put in an incredible amount of overtime in their final year.

A lid of sorts was put on the pension bonanza in 1973. Under the New York State Constitution, no pension benefit, once granted, can be reduced. But nonuniform people hired since 1973 must now wait until age 62 to get their full pension benefits. New garbagemen retiring after 25 years can get only a maximum of 60 percent of the first $12,000 of their final "base salary" and 50 percent of the rest. This partial lid expires next year and the city's unions plan to fight renewal.

Not surprisingly, New York's total pension costs, including Social Security, have jumped from $361 million in 1965 to the current $1 billion-plus in 1974. And that tab could easily double, to $2 billion, within the next five years. Dr. Bernard Jump, a professor with the Metropolitan Studies Program at Syracuse University, has been studying the city's pension mess for several years. He recently revealed that even if the city fires or retires thousands of workers and freezes all wages and benefits for the rest of the decade, its pension costs will still be close to $1.5 billion by 1980—almost a 50 percent gain over 1974. That alone would be double the city's current deficit. Although the city's response to its current budget crisis may pare these projections, most of this obligation has already been promised to employees on the payrolls or pension rolls.

By law, the city's pensions must be fully funded and the actuarial tables must be updated every five years. In reality, the actuarial assumptions haven't been revised since World War I. Funding is based on 1908 to 1914 mortality rates and salary increases, increases that ran about 1.5 percent a year.

Says Dr. Jump: "New York City's actuarial retirement systems are substantially underfunded." How much? Nobody can really know until the actuarial assumptions are updated. One city official told FORBES, "Nobody around here *wants* to know."

The city in 1968 committed itself to paying an extra $126 million a year for the next 35 years—more than $4 billion altogether—to make up for past underfunding. But it didn't reform the pension system itself, nor did it update those actuarial tables to find out the true extent of the underfunding.

Instead, according to the New York State Pension Commission, a state-appointed panel, the underfunding has worsened since then by almost $2 billion as a result of a variety of budgetary gimmicks. For example, in 1971, when teacher benefits were improved, the city virtually stopped contributing to their pension fund for two years for "administrative reasons," thereby "saving" itself $225 million.

Incredibly, there are many public employee pension funds in worse shape than New York City's. The Massachusetts system, for instance, has no assets, whereas New York's does contain $7 billion in investments. (City employees can thank their stars that only about 10 percent of this money is in city bonds.) In Massachusetts, all pension benefits are appropriated annually on a "pay-as-you-go" basis. Last fall in a survey of major state and municipal pension systems, *Pensions & Investments* magazine found their systems underfunded by $22 billion. And the real number is probably higher. New York City, presumably straight-faced, told *P&I* that it was fully funded.

What happens next? The taxpayer is in revolt. So is the investor in municipal bonds. Ultimately, in New York and elsewhere, many benefits may have to be sealed back.

New York City will probably be a forerunner for the rest of the country. And sooner rather than later.

This is a lesson: Beware of the politician or the labor leader who promises you a free lunch. ■

June 15, 1975

EPILOGUE: It is true that unlike politicians, businessmen don't have to stand for re-election, but it is equally true that unfunded (and many times undisclosed) pension liabilities are every bit as serious a problem for investors in corporations as for investors in tax-exempt securities. *Businessweek* magazine recently compiled a list of corporations' unfunded pension liabilities (see *Businessweek*, August 14, 1978) and among the most underfunded were: Lockheed ($404 million in unfunded liabilities which came to 184.6 percent of Lockheed's net worth); L-T-V Corp. ($466 million, 121.4 percent of worth); and Bethlehem Steel Corp. ($1.2 billion, 55.6 percent of net worth).

This problem is of more than academic concern. In mid-1978 a FORBES editor noticed that the stock of giant tire-maker UniRoyal Corp. was selling at *one-third* the company's book value. Was Uni-Royal so undervalued, the editor wondered, as to be a real investment opportunity? Considerable digging turned up one possible reason for the steep discount from book value! UniRoyal's unfunded pension liabilities came to $515 million, as against total assets of $1.7 billion and long-term debt of $550 million! (For more about the financial havoc caused at UniRoyal by its pension plans, see FORBES, July 24, 1978).

Now you see it...

As a literary form, the average corporate prospectus is an abysmal failure. No doubt about it. But those who don't at least make a stab at translating that repellent legalese are missing some great entertainment and a lot of revealing insights. At least in our opinion.

Take, for example, the latest prospectus of United Brands (AMK-John Morrell-United Fruit) published to scant critical acclaim on February 15, 1973. Behind 62 pages of dense verbiage lies a tale of rare imagination. A kind of fiscal fairy tale.

At first glance, it appears to be a very routine renegotiation of debt. United Brands offers to take back up to $125 million (face value) of its old 5-1/2 percent convertible subordinated debentures that come due in 1994. It offers in exchange cash and new nonconvertible debentures paying 9-1/8 percent coming due in 1998. For every $100 in face value on the old bonds, the company would give $10 in cash, and $60 in face value on the new, higher interest bonds. Why should the holders trade $100 for $70? Simple. The $100 was worth only about $61 in the actual market. The new cash and bond package would have a higher current value and roughly the same yield.

Nothing very entertaining about that.

Okay. But just read that last line on the short "supplement" attached on March 5 to the front page of the prospectus. That boring bond swap, it appears, will create about $20 million in 1973 aftertax income for United Brands.

A bit more interesting?

Here's a company that sells about $1.7 billion worth of meat, bananas and ice cream, and yet, in the past five years, has only managed to average about

$6.6 million in earnings, after all the special charges and credits. That works out to an annual profit margin in the dismal neighborhood of about .4 percent. Any good supermarket does at least three times as well.

But if United Brands Chairman Eli Black hasn't exactly been a roaring success in the food business, he is pretty good at arithmetic. He reads on November 21 that the Accounting Principles Board has a new rule: As of January 1, 1973, any difference in principal arising from any early extinguishment of debt must be flowed through current earnings in one year.

After reading that, we suppose, Black puts down his newspaper, gets out a pad of paper and does a few quick calculations. Suppose he retired half of the old 5-1/2 percent bonds, about $125 million worth in terms of face value. Theoretically he could buy them back for around $75 million on the open market. If he did, United Brands would be "obliged" under APB Opinion 26 to take the $50-million difference, less expenses, straight into pretax earnings. That's a lot easier than selling bananas.

We could almost see Black wincing at the thought of having to shell out $75 million in real money, however.

But wait a minute! United Brands was paying out about $6.9 million a year in interest on the old bonds at 5-1/2 percent of their $125 million face value. That worked out to an effective interest rate of 9-1/8 percent on their $75 million market value. Suppose the company simply offered its bondholders new bonds with a *face* value of $75 million paying 9-1/8 percent. The bondholders wouldn't lose any interest. United Brands wouldn't have to shell out $75 million. But the company would still add $50 million to current pretax earnings and reduce its debt by $50 million to boot!

Whereupon, we imagine, Black smiles, reaches for the telephone, and tries out his brainstorm on his financial staff and United Brands underwriters. Ah, how the telephone lines must have sizzled as the idea took shape!

Great stuff, Eli! But you've got to sweeten the offer to persuade those bondholders to make the switch. So toss in a little cash, say $12.5 million. In exchange for those greenbacks, you might also get the bondholders to give up the conversion feature—although with your stock at 9-1/2, conversion at 55 is hardly a threat. And you could tack on, say, four years to the bond's maturity date.

Then, of course, you'll have about $1 million in underwriting costs, plus some miscellaneous costs. Now we don't really know how much tax, if any, you'll have to pay on this deal. Or when. Even if the goverment taxes you at 40 percent, you'll still have a net gain of $20 million. But if your domestic operations run in the red, you might well get it all back in the form of future tax carrybacks.

Net result: no taxes at all, most likely. Which might leave you a net gain of $33 million or so.

Had FORBES accurately reconstructed Black's reasoning? We posed that question to United Brands financial vice president Edward Gibbons, among others in the company, and to Goldman, Sachs partner and UB director Donald Gant. More or less, they said. Well, at least Black was better with bonds than with bananas. Or was he? What about that $20 million (or $33 million)? Was it real?

Not really. Black's $20 million looked more like Chinese money. Simply an accounting adjustment. He was, in effect, laying out $13.5 million now for the chance to save $50 million in sinking fund payments over a weighted average of 15 years. Big deal. If United Brands were profitable enough to earn 9 percent or so on its invested capital, Black could achieve the same result by buying banana boats: $13.5 million in current dollars invested at 9-1/8 percent compounded has exactly the same actuarial value as the $50 million in 15 years. Furthermore, he doesn't even start saving that money until 1980, when sinking fund payments begin: and he doesn't get it all until 1994. But thanks to APB 26, he shows all that gain this year.

Yet the $20 million after taxes are really very future dollars, and worth only a fraction of that amount today.

Of course, Black *had* improved his balance sheet somewhat by reducing long-term debt by $50 million. If that sounds like a lot of money, consider this: Over a fourth of the assets of United Brands, or $281 million, was "goodwill." What this means is that Black paid more for his acquisitions than they were worth on the books. Most of that intangible goodwill, or $252.9 million to be precise, resulted from AMK's 1970 merger with United Fruit—an incredibly high value to attach to the reputation, trademarks and patents of a company that even in a good year when there were no hurricanes had difficulty earning a decent return on its assets.

Now if Black had acquired United Fruit after APB Opinion 17 took effect in November 1970, he would have had to write off that $252.9 million over a maximum of 40 years. Under those circumstances, we supposed, Black would have faced a $6 million a year drain on earnings until the year 2010 instead of showing a $20 million gain in earnings for the year 1973.

Negative Goodwill

But United Brands stated quite clearly on page 53 of the prospectus that the entire $281 million was *not* being amortized at all. It would stay as an "asset." Black wasn't being very consistent here. Back in 1966 he had managed to acquire meatpacker John Morrell for an amount substantially *less* than net asset value, $6.4 million to be exact. Result: Black was taking $641,000 a year into earnings over the ten-year period from 1966 to 1976 in the form of *negative* goodwill. Why do the reverse and charge earnings in order to write off positive goodwill on United Fruit if he didn't absolutely have to?

But maybe we were being too hard on Eli Black. Were we? The question

Paper money

The first few lines of General Host's 1974 income statement sing a mournful song: Pretax income from continuing operations was *down* 25 percent to $4 million. Ah, but General Host's bottom line hums a different tune: Net income for 1974 was *up*—up 300 percent!—to a record of $9.17 per share.

How do you produce higher profits out of lower profits? It's one of the marvels of modern bookkeeping. In this case a nice little gimmick called "gains on extinguishment of debt."

"Extinguishment" is a cute term. It doesn't mean that General Host paid off its debt at less than 100 cents on a dollar and thereby earned a substantial discount. What General Host did was shuffle some pieces of paper and produce a paper profit of nearly $17 million—turning a poor year into a triumphant one. The old paper was "extinguished." New paper was substituted in its place.

It worked like this: Outstanding was $33.9 million in convertible debentures due in 1988, paying 5 percent interest—total annual interest, about $1.7 million. Management offered to swap for it $20.3 million new convertible debentures, paying 11 percent total interest, about $2.2 million. At the same time, the company reduced the conversion price from $27 per common share to $16. The bondholders took the offer. Why not? The holders' current income was enhanced by about 32 percent and conversion terms were improved.

Thus, even though Host's interest expense was increased from $1.7 million to $2.2 million, its books were improved by the wiping out of nearly $13.6 million in debt. And the "profit" came through in 1974, despite the fact that the debt wasn't due.

That is a lot easier way to make money than selling meat and tourism.

was put to Philip Defliese, managing partner of Coopers & Lybrand and head o the Accounting Principles Board. Defliese more than confirmed our suspicions.

"This is precisely the type of thing I was concerned about when I dissented from Opinion 26," he replied.

Then we checked with Abraham Briloff, that tough-minded professor of accounting from Baruch College of the City University of New York. Briloff was much brusquer than Defliese. "The deal," he snorted, "is just so much fiscal masturbation!"

Now you see Eli Black's $50 million.

Now you don't. ■

April 15, 1973

For some peculiar reason, the Financial Accounting Standards Board has put its imprimatur on this exercise in funny finance, calling these gains "extra-ordinary" income—whatever that means. But as Harvard Business School Professor John Shank puts it: "The board didn't raise the basic issue, which is whether this is income at all and in what period."

Boil it down and what you get is this: The company reports a "profit" but incurs a huge increase in interest liability against a very-far-in-the-future reduction in capital liability. Concedes William McHugh, a partner in Coopers & Lybrand: "They've effectively taken a profit this year and will pay it back over the life of the new bonds, through increased charges to future income." Is this what the accounting board calls clearer and more straightforward accounting?

"We're on the horns of a dilemma here," agrees Frank T. Weston, partner of Arthur Young & Co. Weston believes that the only solution to the dilemma is adoption of current value accounting, under which changes in the market value of debt would be recognized as they occur. On the other hand, Philip Defliese, managing partner of Coopers & Lybrand, dissented from the accounting board's ruling in this matter, wanting to see the "profit" amortized over the life of the bonds so that the price paid for the gain would be increased interest in subsequent periods. But he was overruled.

General Host is quick to point out that it didn't invent the gimmick. The ruling is that of the FASB. Nor is General Host the only company to take advantage of this murky provision. Grumman did too last year. Gulf & Western got 19 percent of its reported profits in 1973 that way. Western Union Corp. played the game. In Eli Black's time, United Brands was big on "extinguishment."

Why shouldn't companies be made to amortize the gain, the way Defliese suggested? It seems a mockery to have profit statements—which most investors think reflect the company's health—embellished with "profits" from paper shuffling. ■

July 1, 1975

EPILOGUE: A few months after "Now you see it. . ." was published, United Brands chairman Eli Black committed suicide by jumping from the window of his Manhattan office. But by no means did discounted debt exchanges end with the tragic incident.

In 1977 Meshulam Ricklis, chairman of Rapid-American Corp., a New York headquarted conglomerate with over $2 billion in sales, exchanged $204 million in old 6 percent sinking fund debentures due in 1988 for $153 million in new 10-3/4 percent sinking fund debentures due in 2003. The income statement effect:

Hypoed Income: Some companies retire, others swap debt.

Company	Type of Ex-tinguishment	Gain (millions)	Pretax Income (millions)	Gain as % of Income	Recent Stock Price	P/E Ratio
Allen Group	Exchange	$ 1.4	$ 5.7	25%	7-5/8	9
GAF	Retirement	5.5	56.0	10	10-5/8	5
General Host	Exchange	16.9*	20.8	81	7-1/4	1
Grumman	Exchange	9.3†	49.8	19	17-1/2	6
McCulloch Oil	Exchange	0.8	5.1	16	5-3/8	22
Pacific Gas & Elec	Retirement	20.0**	293.5	7	20-1/4	7
Pan East Pipe	Retirement	4.2**††	103.8	4	29-1/4	6
Trans World Air	Retirement	2.7**	(22.8)	–	7-3/8	–
UAL	Retirement	20.6	224.0	9	18-5/8	6

*Includes $751,000 debt retirement. † No income tax paid or gain. **Gain result of sinking fund requirement. †† Gain is being amortized, under Federal Power Commission accounting change January 1, 1974.

an "extraordinary credit" to profits of $30 million—just for shuffling paper around. Without the gain from the debt exchange, Rapid-American's fiscal 1978 fully diluted earnings-per-share would have been $1.83, a slight increase from the year-earlier $1.43 per share. But *with* the "extraordinary credit," Rapid's net income jumped to $5.11 per share—for a thumping year-to-year earnings gain of 250 percent!

Moral: Don't expect a complete story from any single financial number— *especially* "net income."

And the beat goes on. In April 1978, Rapid-American announced it would exchange $55 million in new 12 percent sinking fund debentures for $72 million of old 7.5 percent debentures. If holders traded in their old notes (they didn't), the extraordinary gain would come to about $17 million. Nor is Rapid-American Corp. the only company whose reported profits are rising in part thanks to early retirements of discounted debt.

Many accountants are clearly embarrassed. Says a ranking partner of Big Eight CPA firm Peat Marwick Mitchell & Co., "Aside from FASB Statement No. 8, reporting profits on debt exchanges is probably the profession's biggest embarrassment." Agrees a Coopers & Lybrand partner: "Unfortunately, APB Opinion 26 is still on the books, and FASB Statement No. 4 says to treat (debt) exchange gains as 'extraordinary.' I personally think it's wrong, but we must follow the rules set down." According to an FASB staff member, the entire matter remains under consideration, but without high priority.

6

THE TRANSLATION OF FOREIGN CURRENCIES

The "Numbers Games" of the preceding three sections have been strung together by a common idea, namely, that assigning values to assets and liabilities is a tricky and potentially misleading business. Now for even worse news: the task becomes exponentially more difficult when the assets and liabilities belong to multinational companies operating in times characterized, as the late 1960s and 1970s have been, by quantum shifts in relative values of the world's leading currencies. (For example: The U.S. dollar is worth about half as many Swiss francs as in 1968; it bought 360 Japanese yen in 1970 but less than 200 in 1978.) Yet increasingly the world economy is dominated by multinational corporations whose foreign assets and liabilities *must*, some way or another, be measured and translated into parent country currency values.

The sticky question of course is: How?

In October 1975, the FASB attempted to answer this question with FASB Statement No. 8, "Accounting for the Translation of Foreign Currency Transactions and Foreign Currency Financial Statements." Statement No. 8 did indeed set rules for how the translation should proceed, and in so doing steeped the FASB in heated and occasionally vitriolic controversy. In 1978 the editors of FORBES noted that FASB No. 8 with no apparent *economic* justification, had knocked down Royal/Dutch Shell's reported profits by some $500 million. The editors awarded the FASB a 1978 FORBES Dubious Achievement Award to the FASB for Statement No. 8, (See FORBES, May 15, 1978.)

A warning: Like the problem it attempts to resolve, Statement No. 8 is highly theoretical and hideously complex. It helps if you keep in mind what FASB No. 8 does. The rule says that certain assets and liabilities must be translated at *current* exchange rates, other assets and liabilities at *historical* exchange rates. Balance sheet valuation differences arising from the translation process must be flowed, as gains or losses, though the income statement.

Does something sound familiar here? Of course. The root problem in the hassle over foreign currency translation is our old friend: How to classify and value *any* asset or liability. Do we measure the value of that Japanese factory by the yen required initially to purchase it—historical cost, in other words? If so do we translate those yen at current exchange rates? Or rates prevailing when the factory was purchased? Or what about that long-term debt? Should we translate it at exchange rates prevailing currently, or rates in effect when the debt was incurred? Are there better solutions that no one has yet come upon?

As you read the following two pieces as well as other articles about FASB Statement No. 8—you might ask yourself: Can the foreign currency translation dilemma *truly* be resolved before the accountants grapple with the underlying problem of how to value assets and liabilities in the first place?

Alice in Accountingland

Or, how strict adherence to accounting logic can produce wrongheaded financial reports.

It's sad but true. In trying to make financial reports reflect economic reality, the accountants sometimes end up making the distortions worse. It's not really their fault. The fact is that "reality," "truth" are elusive things. Listen to the sad case of ICN Pharmaceuticals, Inc., a California-based multi-national drug company with some $180 million sales.

In 1971 ICN expanded into Germany, borrowing deutsche marks long term to buy a company. The company prospered, throwing off deutsche marks to amortize the debt. Without having to put in any actual capital, ICN would end up with a valuable asset. A good investment, right?

Wrong, said the 1974 financial statement. It told shareholders that ICN *lost* about $5 million on the deal, a "foreign currency translation loss" that helped pound ICN's earnings into the red. (And that's not to mention further "losses" on other foreign currency translations.)

How can a *good* investment produce such *bad* results? The answer lies in the bookkeeping. A recent Financial Accounting Standards Board exposure draft would, if accepted by the accounting fraternity, force all multinationals to keep their books the way ICN keeps its books—and with potentially confusing results.

ICN has already adopted this kind of bookkeeping. It requires that foreign *debts* be handled in one way and foreign *assets* in quite another. The debts must be converted to dollars at the exchange rate prevailing on the closing date of the balance sheet period. Assets, on the other hand, are converted at the rate which prevailed when they were first brought onto the books.

Take a simple example. A company buys a German factory in 1965 and pays DM 100 million; at that time the DM is, say, four to the dollar. So the factory is on the books at $25 million.

Now let's look at the other side of the balance sheet. Supposing—as ICN did—the purchase price was borrowed in Germany in DM. Supposing, too, for the sake of simplicity, that the loan has not been amortized and remains at DM 100 million. The result would be bookkeeping disaster for the company because the DM has been strong against the dollar. A dollar now buys only about 2.5 DM, not four DM. The company would, under the new rules, have to now carry its DM debt at $40 million, not $25 million. It would have to report the difference, $15 million, as a loss on the income statement.

Yet when you add everything up, nothing has changed for the company in the real world. Sure, it owes more in *dollars*. But it has an asset which, presumably, has appreciated at least as much in dollars. But the loss must go right down to the bottom line. The gain never gets there. So the company makes a good investment, yet shows a loss.

Just that happened to ICN.

Of course, the thing can work in reverse. The case we mentioned was where the dollar was weak against the other currency. Suppose the dollar was strong. Suppose the deal was done not in Germany but in Argentina. In that case, the company would be able to report a big bookkeeping *profit*, because the peso debt would depreciate in dollar terms, but the physical asset would not have to be written down accordingly.

Logic is Logic

Silly? Not so, says the FASB. It argues that foreign currency long-term debt must be viewed as if the U.S. parent company used dollars to borrow, say, deutsche marks, and then shipped the deutsche marks to its German subsidiary. Explains Jules Cassel, director of the FASB's foreign currency translation project: "From a U.S. parent company's point of view, and from a consolidated point of view in our unit of measurement—dollars—there *is* a loss on the debt repayment because it will take more dollars to repay the original DM borrowing.

"Look," the FASB's Cassel goes on, "you have 200 things spread throughout the world. You must select a single unit of measurement to inform the readers of your financial statements of what you have, given the *basis* of measurement and the *unit* of measurement used on that basis." Since the Board was dealing with U.S. companies, it felt the unit of measurement had to be in the U.S. shareholders' financial language—U.S. dollars.

Okay, but why not mark up (or down) the *assets* as well as the *liabilities*? That wouldn't make sense, argues Cassel. Historical cost is historical cost: You can't be constantly changing it. To do so would be a clear violation of generally accepted accounting principles. By these principles, assets are carried at what they originally cost, not what they may or may not be worth today. "Under generally accepted accounting principles," Cassel says, "the value of the factory is not recognized in the financial statement. We're under historical cost, not current value accounting."

Technically speaking, Cassel is right. But does it make sense, practically speaking, to require a corporation to report a loss where, in fact, it made a profit? Or vice versa?

On this, the accounting fraternity is divided. Arthur Young's Donald J. Hayes, who opposes the exposure draft, thinks it makes no sense to treat liabilities one way, assets another. "We feel," Hayes said, "that to come up with an accounting answer that's consistent with the economics of a currency realignment, the current exchange rate should be applied to all the company's assets and liabilities. The FASB's draft tends to produce results inconsistent with the real economics of what is happening." In other words, you should adjust both sides of the balance sheet for currency changes.

In the real world, of course, the situation isn't quite as cut and dried as these theoretical arguments make it seem; the ICN case is rather a special one. In the real world, the dollar isn't always weak, and so the multinationals may gain as much in reported earnings as they lose. In other words, if the new system created absurdities, it would also produce offsetting absurdities. Overall, it would be a case of a series of wrongs making a single right. Assuming, of course, a company is sufficiently large to have enough wrongs working for it.

And if the company only operates in a few countries? It can avoid the problem by purchasing foreign currency contracts equal to the size of its foreign currency debt. If debt gets written up, so does the contract. But, asks Daniel Lundy of Coopers & Lybrand, "Why should a company be forced to spend money to insure against risks that may exist only in accountants' minds? It's a classic case of the tail wagging the dog!"

One Fell Swoop

Still, what *really* worries corporation executives—as opposed to accountants—is the provision in the FASB's proposal that requires that the write-downs —or write-ups—be reflected in the precise year the currency changes occurred. Dow Chemical, for example, follows the practice of adjusting its debts to reflect currency changes. But Dow spreads the profit or loss over the life of the debt. It's one thing to take a currency adjustment of that sort in a single year and quite another to spread it over, say, 20 years.

We at FORBES sympathize with the accountants. We applaud their efforts to make companies put the facts of currency gains and losses right out on the table where everybody can see them. But is disclosure really disclosure if it ends up making the situation muddier than it was in the beginning? As we said at the start of this article: Everybody wants to get at the truth, but truth is not easily reduced to a set of generally accepted accounting principles. ∎

April 15, 1975

The nightmare
of FASB-8

Thanks to this grotesque ruling, even reading the fine print won't always help you figure out how your companies are really doing.

If you don't know what a mess FASB-8 has created, try this: IBM and ITT, among other major corporations, have taken opposing positions on compliance, and ITT's comptroller, Herbert C. Knortz, who is a leading advocate of full compliance, is also a leading advocate of total repeal. FASB-8, of course, is Financial Accounting Standards Board Statement No. 8, the one requiring corporations to report the effects of foreign currency fluctuations on their results.

The controversy over what ought to be reported to shareholders hangs on the word "practicable" as applied to reporting the effects of currency fluctuations on a company's profit and loss statement. ITT's Knortz says that it is indeed practicable to report currency translation effects on the P&L statement as well as on the balance sheet, adding, "It is always determinable to exactly the same degree that the balance sheet is." Companies that don't comply fully, he says, "are not telling the whole story." At the same time, Knortz calls FASB-8 "one of the most extreme and devastating situations in accounting."

Is he talking out of both sides of his mouth? Not exactly. It's just that he figures that if everybody disclosed the whole story, a lot more companies would join in the pressure to throw out the ruling altogether. So his two-way position makes sense.

IBM's statement to FORBES is typical of companies that don't agree with Knortz about income-statement reporting: "Effects of the [currency] rate changes on reported revenues, costs and expenses cannot be quantified with any precision and accordingly are not reported. To quantify this effect would assume that all other factors involved in foreign operations are not affected by currency values and that no compensatory changes are made. It doesn't consider the resulting economic effects of possible volume and price changes and expense level changes."

From a sampling of annual reports, FORBES finds that relatively fewer companies seem to be reporting both income-statement and balance-sheet changes than report balance-sheet changes only. Along with ITT, full disclosers include Kraft, Inc. On the other hand, Exxon, Caterpillar Tractor, Standard Oil of California, Xerox and Black & Decker show only balance-sheet effects. Another group, including Eastman Kodak and Avon Products, reported both until the current year and then went to balance-sheet effects only.

To make matters worse, corporations report the required currency translations according to their own interpretations of the ruling.

Consider ITT's second-quarter report for this year. It showed a balance-sheet loss of 20 cents per share from foreign-currency effects for this year's first half. The income statement translation showed a 56-cents-per-share *gain*. The company's entire 36-cent earnings increase this year is attributable to FASB-8 accounting adjustments.

Compare this with Eastman Kodak Co., which disclosed translation changes for both statements until this year. In its first-quarter 1978 stockholder report, however, the company omitted the income statement translation without explanation. Its earnings per share were up 50 percent; 87 cents compared with 58 cents for last year's first quarter. Of the company's $16-million foreign-currency loss for last year's first quarter, $15.6 million derived from the income statement. But because Kodak now discloses only the balance-sheet effect, investors will be unable to determine what portion of this year's earnings are from the income statement translation.

Kodak's per-share earnings of $2.06 for this year's first half amounted to a 45 percent increase over last year's $1.42. A recent press release about higher

Discrepant Disclosure

ITT

Foreign Currency Translation: Net foreign exchange gains (losses) arising from the conversion of foreign currencies and the translation of balance sheet items are included in income and amounted to $4,103,000 and $(46,000) for 1977 and 1976, respectively. In addition, translation of the 1977 income statement at average rates of exchange that differed from those used in the prior year affected earnings favorably by $890,000.

IBM

A foreign currency exchange gain of $28 million, consisting principally of unrealized gains from the translation of foreign currency assets and liabilities, was included in 1977 net earnings.

No two examples better illustrate conflicting FASB-8 disclosure parctices than these paragraphs from the 1977 annual reports of International Telephone & Telegraph Corp. and International Business Machines Corp. ITT shows currency translation effects on both balance sheet and income statement; IBM, only on the balance sheet.

sales for the company's international photographic division states: "Favorable foreign exchange rates and somewhat higher prices also contributed to the increase." Yet the company showed an "exchange loss" of $13.3 million for the first six months of this year. It is obvious that undisclosed income-statement foreign-currency gains offset the balance-sheet losses. But an investor has no way of knowing how much Kodak benefited from this.

How can an investor make any sense out of financial reporting in this morass of inconsistency? Who is reporting properly: ITT or Kodak and IBM? The Financial Accounting Standards Board won't take a stand, though it acknowledges that some U.S. multinationals are less than forthright in their reporting practices. With all this confusion, it's no surprise that the FASB is being flooded with complaints calling for the repeal of Statement No. 8 since its adoption in 1975.

Aggravating the problem in recent months has been the dollar's plunge against major foreign currencies. Companies with major operations where local currency is rising against the dollar—in Germany or Switzerland, for example—are showing big earnings increases.

The rule requires that companies carry inventories, fixed assets and depreciation at historical exchange rates and most other financial statement items at current rates. This means that controllers and treasurers have to contend with the additional distortions of mismatched assets and liabilities, sales and inventories. If the dollar declines relative to the mark, let's say, *sales* for that foreign subsidiary would be translated into more dollars, but inventories could remain locked into last year's rate when the dollar was stronger. The sales gain would be magnified and the company would report a larger earnings gain than was strictly justified.

Recently, the Treasury Department launched a study to determine whether Statement No. 8 has increased the dollar's instability by encouraging corporate treasurers to hedge in foreign exchange markets to offset reporting distortions. But the real issue is this: If the FASB can't enforce consistency in disclosure, it should scrap the rule altogether because it seems to be confusing a situation that it was supposed to clarify. ■

September 18, 1978

EPILOGUE: Nearly everyone agrees that Statement No. 8 is the FASB's single most troublesome ruling. Yet as *Forbes' Numbers Game* goes to press, the FASB continues to adhere to the rule as it was published in October 1975; in April 1976, the Board formally voted *not* to reconsider the rule. Why the steadfastness? Here is how the FASB's thoughtful Chairman Donald Kirk put the problem to partners of CPA firm Main Lafrentz & Co. late in 1978:

I'd say that accountants haven't agreed on how to handle currency translation since the problem first arose. And I doubt if accountants are ever going to be fully satisfied with any particular standard the Board issues on this subject. There is no way we can keep accountants from arguing about what the best approach might be to various problems that arise. Clearly Statement No. 8 has been widely criticized. It is a complex subject that is very difficult to explain. Solutions to the problem are limited, and none of them will satisfy everybody. It's one thing to criticize Statement No. 8—that's easy—but it's another thing altogether to suggest a workable solution.

The FASB is now scrutinizing the controversial rule and may amend it soon. One reason it may do so is that there appear to be real and perhaps undesirable economic costs spawned by the Statement No. 8. In December 1978, the FASB published "The Impact of FASB-8 on the Foreign Risk Management Practices of American Multinationals," by University of South Carolina Professors Thomas G. Evans, William R. Folks, Jr., and Michael Jilling. The trio investigated foreign exchange risk management practices at 157 major U.S. multinational corporations in the wake of FASB-8. Among their findings:

"There exists the belief that FASB Statement No. 8 causes American financial management to overemphasize the reported earnings impact of foreign exchange gains and losses as compared to other financial considerations. . ."

"Almost 84 percent of the respondents believed that currently prevailing accounting principles (i.e., FASB Statement No. 8) misleads management, stockholders, and security analysts. Over 60 percent agreed that they need a more flexible translation method than Statement No. 8. . ."

"Sixty-eight percent of the management surveyed believed that current accounting principles do not allow a satisfactory measure of the total effect of an exchange rate change. An even larger number believed that the translation practices of FASB Statement No. 8 do not result in an accurate measure of the firm's actual exposure to exchange risk. . ."

"Slightly less than 50 percent of the firms that now purchase foreign exchange forecasts from outside consultants began purchasing after FASB Statement No. 8 became effective. . ."

"There is evidence that firms have substantially accelerated their dividend flows from weak currency foreign subsidiaries to reduce exposure. . ."

"Since January 1, 1976 firms have reduced borrowing in the German mark and Swiss franc, increased borrowing in the British pound, Canadian dollar, French franc, and Mexican peso, and remained at the same level in the Japanese yen. . ."

Said an FASB staff member at about the time the Statement study was released: "We know we have a major problem with Statement No. 8 and we know we must move forward expeditiously."

7 HOW NOT TO BE TAKEN

Is there a point to putting in the time and sweaty effort required to understand financial statements? Why *bother* laboring over the arcane rules and philosophies that govern how economic enterprises report their economic successes and failures?

There is a point, of course, and the point is the title of this section of *Forbes Numbers Game: How Not To Be Taken.* The point, in other words, is to understand the rules of financial accounting well enough to beat the other fellows—or at least not be taken by them—in the game of financial numbers. In a sense that's what "The Numbers Game" articles are all about.

Are you an accountant or a would-be accountant? Then you should know how accountants and accounting rules in the past may have failed to protect the public from being taken in by unscrupulous managements; thus will you avoid their mistakes (and perhaps their legal defense costs). Are you an investor or potential investor? Then you should know how your peers have been taken by unscrupulous managements aided perhaps indirectly and unknowingly by sleepy accountants. Are you an unscrupulous manager (or would-be one)? Then you'll want to know how *your* peers have taken investors and accountants in the past; thus may you create new ways to pull balance sheets over the eyes of the unwary in the future.

More explicit than "The Numbers Games" that have gone before, the following pieces are full of practical advice on keeping other peoples' unwanted hands off your coin. On pages 139-142 you'll discover what a Form 10-K is and how it might save you from a collapsing company *before* the roof falls in. A Form 8-K, too, could help you keep up with the Smart Money. What's a Form 8-K? See "Nothing to hide" (page 143).

The final article in this section, "How to keep from being taken," is a wrap-up piece. It was written in 1970 and so in one level is a rather charming period piece that brings to life some of the financial "high-jinkery" that was part and parcel of the late 1960s go-go euphoria. But the story is more than a slice of history: Many of the accounting abuses available in 1970 are still on the shelves. Interestingly enough—or depressingly enough, take your choice—"How not to be taken" is as fresh and as full of apt advice today as it was nearly a decade ago.

Figuring out footnotes

"How do you read an annual report—intelligently, I mean?"

There was no ducking the question, difficult as it was, for it came from a promising young man who had just joined our staff.

"I've got an MBA, and I majored in economics at college, but I still don't get as much out of these things as I think I should. What's the secret?"

Well, as any serious investor knows, you read them backwards, we replied.

"Backwards?"

We reached across the desk and picked up a copy of Honeywell's 1973 annual report, which had just arrived with the morning's mail.

You start with the auditor's letter at the end of the financial statements to see if its qualified, we explained. If the last sentence—the one that begins "In our opinion"—contains the words "subject to," you know right away that the outside accountants have serious misgivings about something in the financial statements. Lockheed's 1972 annual report had a "subject to" saying that about $1 billion of L-1011 aircraft inventory might never be sold. An important warning.

And sometimes you'll find an "except for" qualifier in that last sentence, we went on. You run into that when a company switches from one acceptable accounting method to another equally acceptable method—as when Kroger switched in 1973 from LIFO (last-in, first-out) to FIFO (first-in, first-out) inventory accounting. The auditor letter alerted you to a footnote to the effect that the change boosted their earnings by over 50 percent.

Now let's see what Haskins & Sells has to say about Honeywell. Nothing. Honeywell got a "clean" opinion—which, of course, is what you'd expect. The great majority of companies do.

"What's next?" asked our young colleague. "The president's letter?"

No, no. You continue reading backwards. Next, you look at the footnotes. They'll often tell you things the president's letter carefully glosses over.

All right, now *here's* something interesting, we continued. Near the start of Honeywell's "Summary of Significant Accounting Policies"—a required disclosure—we see the company has an unconsolidated finance subsidiary.

"Excuse me, but why is that interesting?"

Well, because that tells you Honeywell is doing some "off-balance-sheet financing." Look, you have to bear in mind what type of company you're dealing with. Honeywell's traditional business is control systems, but the company now gets about half its revenues from computers. Now what do you suppose is the critical factor in a highly competitive field like computers—aside from technology?

"Well, let's see, it's a capital-intensive business. And lots of your revenues come from rentals or leases rather than sales. Your income gets spread out over several years. So I guess it would be capital."

Very good. Now back to this finance subsidiary. IBM has such a fat income stream from its base of heavily depreciated leased equipment that it is a net cash generator. But Honeywell probably isn't. So they have to get cash by borrowing against their leases. The finance subsidiary does that, and in the process it should generate a lot of debt that doesn't show up on the parent's balance sheet. Here it is in footnote 5.

Sure, look at that debt! Honeywell's finance subsidiary increased its long-term debt last year by $75 million, to $125 million.

We turned back to the parent company balance sheet.

See? If you had looked first at their consolidated balance sheet, you might have thought that long-term debt increased by only $28 million, to $386 million. But we know that's not right. In fact, Honeywell's long-term debt increased over $100 million last year if we include their finance subsidiary.

"But why do they bother to keep them separate?" asked our young friend, looking over our shoulder. "Even if they did consolidate that finance subsidiary. total equity of about $1.2 billion would still amount to 55 percent of capitalization. That's not that much lower than the 62 percent they show now. And they probably don't earn as high a return in their finance subsidiary as they do in their main business, do they?"

You're right, they don't, we replied. They have, let's see, a 5 percent rate of return in that finance subsidiary compared with an 11 percent return in the basic business. But a finance company can operate with a high ratio of debt to equity. Honeywell's finance subsidiary, for example, has total debt that's 2.6 times its equity base.

"So it's a way of stretching your borrowing power."

Partly, but that's not the only advantage. The finance company can balance short-term commercial paper and long-term obligations and get better interest rates than Honeywell could negotiate directly.

"Smart move. But what did they do with that extra $75 million in long-term debt that the subsidiary borrowed?

Okay, here it is. They had $113 million in short-term commercial paper borrowings in that subsidiary, and they used this long-term borrowing to roll over commercial paper into 25-year long-term debt. Prudent, given the sharp rise in the commercial paper rate last year.

Anyway, you see, by reading the footnotes first you can tell that Honeywell is playing a pretty sophisticated game. Look at note 3, for example, which shows when all borrowings come due. A nice steady stream of maturities there. No big "balloon" payments.

Now, let's see how they use that financial subsidiary. A little farther down in the accounting policies footnote, they tell us that they recognize earnings on leased computers as the money comes in over the life of the lease. That's conservative. Since they must need more cash than this actually produces, they sell some of the receivables from these leases to the subsidiary. Honeywell gets dollars it can use instead of lease commitments, and the subsidiary raises cash to buy the receivables by going into the money market and borrowing on the lease income.

"Well, but isn't that a chance for some fancy footwork? When they assign those leases to the subsidiary, do they then recognize the future income even though payment hasn't been made?"

Good question, we replied. There's potential for what's politely called "managing earnings." But the accountants won't allow it. They now have strict rules governing the recognition of lease income. By transferring those future leases, Honeywell gets the money borrowed against them for use as working capital. The summary of changes in financial position shows that this produced about $50 million last year. But that money doesn't get reported on the income statement. Instead, it appears on the balance sheet as a liability in the form of deferred rental income.

All right, now let's quick check through the rest of these notes here. Their inventories are on first-in, first-out. . .

"Just like most companies."

Besides, the whole computer industry is on FIFO. Ideally, none of them should be—that's just one man's opinion.

Okay. They expense research and developmnent costs as incurred, which is conservative. Oops! Wait a minute. They have a couple of exceptions here that could be important. Remember Memorex? Their financial difficulties last year stemmed in part from $28 million in capitalized research and development that had to be written off when they couldn't sell the products.

Let's take a look at those exceptions. All right, they capitalize R&D on cost-plus government contracts. No problem there since the future income to offset the expense is assured. But now in the second exception they say they capitalize R&D expense on "hardware engineering and product development expenses assigned to computer systems used internally, leased to customers or in the process of manufacture."

"That sounds like *all* computer R&D."

Not quite so fast, we warned. The note mentions only *hardware-related* expenses which are capitalized; R&D for computer *software* is expensed. Unfortunately, we don't know how much money is involved.

We flipped through the glossy pictures and text to see if Honeywell's annual report gave a figure for total R&D commitments. Here, on page 21. They spent $269 million last year.

"But how much was capitalized?"

Who knows? You can see that reading the notes raised another good question. Probably only a small portion of that amount, but they don't tell us.

We proceeded. Depreciation . . . good will . . . nothing significant there. Computers are written off over a five-year period, which seems reasonable. Goodwill—that's the premium over asset value that Honeywell has paid for acquisitions—is less than 2 percent of total assets. So we won't worry about what they bought. Foreign operations . . . again no problem. The note says exchange adjustments weren't material.

Income taxes? According to Honeywell's income statement, the company is actually paying about $36 million less in taxes than it reports. The difference shows up on the balance sheet as a deferred liability. In other words, income for tax purposes is about $72 million lower than the figure reported in the income statement.

"Is that possible?"

Oh, certainly, we said. Just about every company keeps two sets of books. One for the tax collector; one for the stockholders. The note here explains that the difference results from things like taking advantage of accelerated depreciation for tax purposes and writing off some of that capitalized R&D we just discussed. That's normal enough.

But watch for big changes in the size of tax deferrals. They could indicate that there has been an accounting switch somewhere that has made a significant impact on the income statement. Honeywell's deferral is about the same size as it was the previous year, so we won't worry.

There *is* an important tax item, though. A little further down in footnote 7 we see that Honeywell has foreign tax-loss carryforwards of $210 million. Now, let's see, this applies only to French income tax. Okay, they're taking advantage of prior years' losses in a French computer company they got when they acquired the assets of GE's computer business in 1970. And they're going to use that loss to offset tax on future income earned in France.

Here, it shows up as an extraordinary item on the income statement—34 cents a share out of a total of $5.46 earned last year. And they go on to say that French law lets this loss carryforward stay on the books indefinitely until it's used up, unlike our tax code which allows similar carryforward only for a five-year period.

"So the tax loss is really sort of a long-term asset that doesn't show up on the balance sheet?"

Right, we said. Assuming, of course, that Honeywell eventually makes enough money in France to offset it. And assuming the French don't change their tax laws.

"I can see why they want to keep it off the balance sheet."

We took a quick look at the last note, contingencies and commitments. The important thing here was the listing of long-term leases and rental agreements. In a sense these represent a form of disguised borrowing. By leasing, they don't tie up as much of their own needed capital in real estate. But, like any other form of leverage, this entails greater risk. Payments on those leases—$31 million this year—are fixed costs just like interest on borrowed money.

And that's about it, we said, sliding Honeywell's annual report back across the desk of our young friend.

"To read an annual report the way you just did you obviously have to know quite a bit about the company and its industry—not to mention accounting."

Well, sure. You have to do a little work, you know. If you're an investor and you're going to put your hard-earned money into this company, isn't it worth doing a little homework first?

"You've raised more questions than you've answered."

That's the whole point! For investors as well as for reporters. ∎

May 1, 1974

B

Whose stamp of approval?

A little over a year ago, much to everyone's surprise, Gulf Oil abruptly backed out of its $850-million deal to acquire CNA Financial Corp. A day later the reason seemed clear: CNA, following the second-highest first-half profits in its history, announced it was suddenly in the red for the third quarter. And in the red to stay, as it turned out. CNA has lost a total of $79 million during the last 12 months.

Odd, isn't it? The first two quarterlies indicate all is well, but the third has a very different story to tell. Was it that CNA's business suddenly and unexpectedly fell off from June 30 on? Not at all. The events that caused the red ink were there all along. A giant real estate subsidiary, the Larwin Group, was in deep trouble. Only management hadn't told stockholders about it. Gulf, checking the books prior to merger, apparently found what stockholders didn't yet know. Gulf closed the books and walked away from the deal. Stockholders were not so lucky.

This is not an isolated case. Again and again stockholders have been lulled into security by good quarterly reports, only to be told later that the reports weren't really accurate. The trouble is this: Interim reports are not audited or certified by the outside accountants; they are *management's* own estimates of the situation. It's not that the accountants are more upright than management; it's just that management frequently has a very strong motive for hiding a mess or hoping that it will go away. It's the accountant's job to save management from such temptation.

Although a good many horses have already been stolen, the accountants are finally moving to close the barn door: not *lock* it, just close it a bit. Coopers & Lybrand, one of the Big Eight accounting firms, was the first to move.

Coopers has a blue-chip client list, including American Telephone & Telegraph, Ford, and Alcoa. It would offer not a full audit of quarterly reports (audits cost too much and take too long) but a *review* of the information accompanied by a letter to stockholders saying that the review had taken place. It wouldn't *certify* the interim report, but would at least give it a limited endorsement.

We began by citing the CNA case. But this was only one of many. Recently Chase Manhattan Corp. stockholders were caught in the same mousetrap. It had reported nice earnings gains for the first two quarters of the year, only to take it all back when a discrepancy was found in its bond-trading account. Queried by FORBES, a Chase executive conceded that a review by the auditors would have uncovered the discrepancy earlier and thus saved Chase a good deal of embarrassment.

The present Mattel situation is an extreme case of what can happen when stockholders have only management's word for interim results. Mattel, the big toymaker, stands accused by the Securities & Exchange Commission of issuing false quarterly reports in 1972. According to the SEC, although Mattel was aware of negative financial information, including the fact that it had a good deal of obsolete inventory, Mattel did not reflect the facts in its quarterly statements. Only at the year's end did it write off the bad inventories—clearly under pressure from its auditors, Arthur Andersen & Co. Early the following year the stockholders learned the bitter truth.

There are many ways that a management can pretty up quarterly statements. Receivables can be booked to profit, even though management is aware that some of them may not be collectible. (National Student Marketing was the classic example.) Or, an obsolete plant can be shut down in January but its write-off delayed until the year's end. Companies can estimate tax rates on the low side during the early quarters, thereby making year-to-year comparisons look favorable. And gross profit margins can be optimistically estimated.

Then there was the Memorex situation. Memorex had been leasing its equipment to customers. In mid-1970, however, it began *selling* the equipment to a controlled but nonconsolidated leasing "subsidiary." Although the real-world situation had not changed—the customers were still leasing—management had created a fictional change. By selling the equipment to its leasing "subsidiary," it was able to book the full profit at once instead of taking it over the life of the leases. The result was a big bulge in Memorex' profits in 1970's third quarter. The auditors, Arthur Andersen, refused to accept the resulting figures. Memorex was forced to withdraw the quarterly and replace it with a far more pessimistic one. But for a while stockholders had been basking in a phony rosy glow.

Needless to say, many managements are not happy with the prospect of the additional red tape—and their opposition doesn't always spring from suspicious motives. Such reviews would certainly increase auditing costs, which are already high. For example, International Telephone & Telegraph paid several million dollars to 25 outside auditors worldwide last year. Even interim reviews would probably add one-third to the costs.

Some people feel that the reviews would slow down the issuance of quarterlies and therefore decrease their costliness. However, John C. Burton, the SEC's crusading chief accountant, thinks this need not be so. Burton has been suggesting not a full-scale audit, but simply a review of the accounting policies used in the quarterlies and the underlying financial statements. This would be a middle ground between a full audit and none at all.

Burton concedes that many auditors are worried about exposing themselves even further to lawsuits, but adds that a good many companies (ITT, Gulf, and Chrysler, for example) already have their auditors informally reviewing their interim reports. Burton thinks making this procedure obligatory and more extensive would reduce the temptation to cut corners by a minority of corporations: "It would bring the bottom group up to par."

Incidentally, FORBES is more than a little proud of its role in bringing this situation to public attention. When we were probing into it recently, we put a question to Philip L. Defliese, Coopers & Lybrand's managing partner, which was: "What could CPAs do to make interim statements more trustworthy?" A few weeks later Coopers & Lybrand announced it was offering a review service that it had been thinking about for over a year. "See what you fellows started," Defliese later said to FORBES' Subrata Chakravarty.

Reviews of interim reports by outside auditors will not, of course, bring about a promised land. It will not save stockholders from unpleasant surprises. What it will do, however, is to make it harder for the surprises to be delayed—a delay that might be useful to insiders but can only be harmful to outside stockholders.

With the stock market in the shape it is, investors can use every bit of confidence and protection that management and their auditors can supply. ∎

November 1, 1974

 **(Expletives deleted)**

Watching the Franklin National Bank situation should have been rather like watching the tail end of a Monopoly game. You remember the scene: The hapless player (read Franklin) lands on Park Place (read Park Avenue). He is asked for enormous rent for his luxurious accommodations. So our unlucky player must tear down his hotels and mortgage his properties to raise cash. In a little over two years, Franklin National reduced its property holdings—from $35 million at the end of 1971 (just before it moved into its new headquarters at 450 Park Avenue) to $14 million at the end of 1973. In 1972 and 1973 it sold $24.5 million worth of buildings and leased them back.

The rest is history—a loss of as much as $39 million in foreign currency transactions and, according to Italian wheeler-dealer Michele Sindona, another loss of $5 million on securities transactions. The bank lost almost a quarter of its deposits in the first five weeks after its problems became public.

How did it all happen so suddenly? Only a month or so before the roof caved in, Franklin had released its 1973 annual report. The cover showed the sun in all its glory against a sky of vivid red, orange and yellow. If ever there was a report bright with hope and promise, it was Franklin's annual report.

Nor was the narrative itself any less optimistic. "Franklin," Chairman Harold V. Gleason reported glowingly to stockholders, "is ideally suited by corporate temperament and tradition to adapt quickly to the vast revolutionary changes anticipated in the new local, national and world order."

Sounds like our bank did all right. Well, there was a disquieting increase in interest expense, from 50 percent of operating expenses in 1972 to 68.5 percent in 1973. But then all banks had that problem in 1973, and accountants

Ernst & Ernst had given the report a "clean" opinion—no caveats; in their opinion the financial statements fairly reflected Franklin's financial condition at the end of 1973.

Alas, then, the stockholders had no warning?

Ah, but they did.   Trouble is that few of them ever get to read a Form 10-K, that detailed document all nationally-traded corporations must file with the Securities & Exchange Commission and which—as we will explain later—is rather hard for the general public to come by although it is a public document.

Banks don't have to file 10-Ks. They are specifically excluded from the requirement. But bank holding companies do. Franklin was a holding company. Implicit in Franklin's 10-K was a corporate horror story, worlds removed from the glossy, happy annual report. No rising sun in the 10-K. Stricly a falling star. Any stockholders who read and understood it might well have bailed out.

Item after item in the 10-K pictured a company unable to keep up with the treadmill it had jumped onto, and seemingly too weary even to step off.

For a start, the 10-K showed that the rise in yield on loans lagged behind the rates the bank had had to pay to acquire the funds. "Indeed," the 10-K continues, "at times during 1973, the rates paid for such funds exceeded the yields earned on such loans."   In other words, there were times when Franklin lost money when it lent money.

There was an item entitled "Federal Funds Borrowed" and another entitled "Other Liabilities For Borrowed Money." These represent highly volatile, very short-term money borrowed by banks, sometimes almost literally overnight. Franklin's annual report showed an increase of 72.5 percent in the purchase of such funds. What it did not show was that the average interest rate Franklin had to pay on those funds was 8.88 percent, a rate higher than the average yield it earned on *any* form of loan outstanding.

Overall, the spread—the difference between the average yield earned and the average rate paid—was a beggarly 0.94 percent, down from 1.91 percent the year before, which was no great shakes itself. If a stockholder had studied these figures he should have been alarmed as interest rates climbed this year. (The overnight rate recently was 12.38 percent.) But he would have looked in vain for such information in the annual report. It was only in the 10-K.

Then the 10-K got to loan losses. The valuation reserve, as the 10-K (but not the annual report) explains, "is the only portion of the reserve available for loan charge-offs." If more loans go sour than the valuation reserve can handle, the balance must come straight out of earnings. Franklin's valuation reserve declined from $20 million in 1969 to $10 million in 1973. In the same period, its loans almost doubled, from $1.5 billion to $2.8 billion. The 10-K writers thought this contrast important enough to emphasize. The annual report didn't mention it at all.

In fact, what the annual report did say on the subject was positively misleading. A footnote in the 1973 annual report states that the year's provision for bad debts actually exceeded by $1 million the minimum amount, which is based on a rolling five-year average of loan-loss experience. Sounds very conservative.

A glance at the 10-K quickly killed this assumption. In mentioning the same transaction, the 10-K pointed out *why* the loan write-off exceeded the formula. The reason was that actual loan losses had also exceeded by $1 million what the formula covered. So, there had been nothing conservative about the bank's accounting. The annual report seemingly tried to make a virtue out of necessity by concealing the reason for the additional charge.

None of these facts—nor many more in the 10-K—came as much of a surprise to the hard-nosed money managers of the big investment houses. With reams of information at their fingertips, they had long since pulled out. "You won't find any sophisticated investors in Franklin National," says Harry Keefe of Keefe, Bruyette & Woods, the bank stock specialists." People who can read a balance sheet were out of there long ago."

The Franklin's report is a tremendous contrast to that of the Security National Bank of Long Island, itself no shining knight when it comes to performance. Security's report is the more commendable because it is not a bank holding company and therefore is not required to file a 10-K. It had the same kinds of problems as did Franklin—negative spreads at times, bad debt losses—but it laid them out clearly in its annual report. And Security's auditors, Arthur Young & Co., gave a qualified opinion to the financial statements because of potentially uncollectible loans due from companies in reorganization. Franklin had such doubtful debts, too, yet Ernst & Ernst did not even require disclosure of them, much less qualify their opinion. The potential losses are mentioned only in the 10-K.

How could Ernst & Ernst have given a clean opinion to such a grotesquely optimistic annual report? How could they have failed to mention the fact that the semiannual examination of the bank, conducted by the Comptroller of the Currency as required by law, had begun in November and had shown no signs of ending at the end of January when the auditors' letter was signed?

We called Ernst & Ernst to ask. They begged off any explanations on the grounds that Franklin was still a client, everybody was being investigated and comment would be inappropriate. So we called Franklin.

We spoke first with Treasurer John Sadlik. After ducking a few questions about the discrepancies between the annual report and the 10-K, Sadlik referred us to the public relations department. "Whatever the differences are, I'm not in a position to comment on them, and I'm not going to discuss them with you," he harrumphed.

Arthur G. Perfall, senior vice president for public relations, was only a bit more helpful. "The annual report does not and is not intended to duplicate the 10-K," he pontificated. "The annual report contains the material which we, and our counsel and our accountants, feel is required and germane." If Franklin made loan decisions the way it apparently expected investors to make investment decisions, no wonder the bank was in trouble.

Dear reader, this isn't really an article about Franklin National. It is really a sermon on the way all too many major corporations regard their annual reports: as a public relations document rather than as an honest accounting to stockholders.

"Let 'em read the 10-Ks," some managements may say. Easier said than done. To get a copy one must either write to the SEC, which will provide one for a fee, or ask the company. It can be time-consuming. We asked Franklin for a 10-K and, after mentioning our affiliation with FORBES, were sent one within a day. But an associate who did not mention FORBES was still waiting a week later.

Any wonder the public has deserted the stock market? ■

July 1, 1974

Nothing to hide

"We don't feel that we had anything to hide," said S. Roy French, secretary and general counsel for Cerro Corp. "We take it that the public will understand that sometimes management and accountants do differ."

In those words the Cerro executive sought to brush aside FORBES' questions about why the company had fired its auditors of 36 years standing, Coopers & Lybrand.

However, we do not brush easily. Not when we have before us 16 pages of a Securities & Exchange Commission document describing eight major disputes between Cerro and its erstwhile auditors.

These documents, called Form 8-K, can be very revealing. In this case they told how Coopers & Lybrand had insisted that Cerro restate its announced 1971 income from $8.5 million down to $2.8 million. They further told how the auditors had insisted on two sweeping "subject to" qualifiers in its certification of the annual reports for 1971 and 1972. These qualifiers suggested that over a third of Cerro's assets—$200 million worth to be precise—might not be recoverable because they were mines located in Chile and Peru, and because of $11.5 million in contingent liabilities on a marginal $1.3-million Australia investment.

Cerro prefers to treat the subsequent change of auditors as just another routine management decision. Lybrand looks at it differently. "I've been in the accounting profession with Coopers & Lybrand for 27 years," said Louis Moscarello, a member of Lybrand's executive committee and the former partner in charge of the Cerro account. "In terms of the diversity of differences, the magnitude of the numbers, and the fact that a press release was issued at a time when we had *not* substantially completed our audit, this was a unique experience for me." Moscarello was referring to Cerro's February 1972 announcement that it had earned—unauditied—$8.5 million in 1971.

One by one, Lybrand's Form 8-K letter ticked off the disputes it had had with Cerro management over the previous 18 months:

- A Canadian subsidiary had lost $3.5 million in 1971. Cerro wanted to take a $1.7-million offset against its U.S. income taxes. Not permissible, said Lybrand.

- Somehow Cerro forgot in 1971 that it had to pay Peruvian income taxes. Lybrand reminded it of that unpleasant fact and insisted upon the creation of a $1.5-million reserve for the purpose.

- Cerro knew it would sustain metal trading losses on its 1971 contracts but had made too small a provision for that. Set aside an additional $391,000, says Lybrand.

- The materials, spare parts and supplies inventory of it's Peruvian Cerro de Pasco subsidiary looked inflated to Lybrand. Over Cerro's objections, Lybrand insisted upon a $1-million pretax charge to income to adjust.

- Cerro's Chilean assets had already been nationalized in 1971. It did not wish to disclose in a footnote that serious discussions touching on possible nationalization were also taking place with the Peruvian government. Lybrand not only insisted upon such disclosure, but included in its certifying letter a strong "subject to" qualification concerning the recoverability of Cerro's investments and assets in Chile, Peru, and Australia.

But the main area of disagreement between Cerro and Lybrand in 1971 had to do with a real estate subsidiary, Leadership Housing Systems. Another accounting firm had already audited Leadership's books and given it a clean opinion. But Lybrand asked Cerro for major documentation of sales contracts and subsequently insisted upon major changes in accounting methods—changes that turned a $758,000 profit into a $1.4-million loss.

In studying Leadership's sales contracts, something it did not have to do, Lybrand discovered, for example, that Leadership was being optimistic, to say the least. It was taking into 1971 earnings a substantial portion of the profits on the sale of six apartment projects to a real estate investment trust under an October agreement. However, construction had not even started on five of them. On several, construction contracts had not even been negotiated.

"They didn't even have a shovel in the ground," said Moscarello. "We felt it was somewhat absurd to recognize profits so soon."

In addition, Lybrand discovered that Leadership was capitalizing normally recurring administrative costs that Lybrand felt should have been charged against income. And Leadership was guaranteeing buyers a certain rate of return on certain income-producing properties, when its own past record in forecasting project costs had proven inaccurate and unreliable.

What Leadership had done was squeak by under "generally accepted" accounting in 1971. But that is just what it was: squeaking by. For the entire field of real estate accounting was rapidly becoming more conservative. Lybrand's fussy position on the real estate accounting question was vindicated by two real estate accounting guides issued by the American Institute of Certified Public Accountants this year.

As Cerro was closing its 1972 books early in 1973, Lybrand again challenged the accounting of Cerro's real estate subsidiary, by now audited by Price Waterhouse as a result of the merger of Leadership and newly acquired Behring Corp. Shortly afterward, Lybrand was fired and Price Waterhouse got the whole Cerro account.

In June, when Price Waterhouse was hired, Cerro Vice President and Controller Paul J. Bennett told Moscarello that the reasons for firing Lybrand were mainly the "agonizing" nature of past differences in financial reporting matters. He conceded that the attitude of Cerro's real estate executives toward what they regarded as Lybrand's nit-picking had been "influential."

To S. Roy French of Cerro, the whole thing amounts to so many sour grapes on Lybrand's part: "Some of the things in their letter to the SEC on Form 8-K go beyond accounting disputes. I think Coopers & Lybrand could be said to have gone considerably beyond what the regulations strictly call for."

One of the things Lybrand talked about was its claim that the audit committee of Cerro's board of directors had not met with Coopers & Lybrand, nor with any of the four accounting firms management was considering as replacements. Lybrand's request to meet with the audit committee had been denied. A Lybrand letter addressed to the Cerro audit committee had never been seen by the chairman of the committee.

Was that what French was referring to?

"Well, that certainly has nothing to do with accounting questions," he replied.

On the contrary, we said, this seems to have a great deal to do with accounting questions. Aren't audit committees supposed to mediate between management and independent auditors when important differences arise? Hadn't Cerro bypassed its own audit committee? Cerro's French replied that the committee members "do not presume to change management's recommendations unless they are dissatisfied with management's steps in analyzing the question of who the auditor should be."

We thought this was a bit beside the point. What are the audit committees for? Certainly not just for rubber stamping management's decisions. They are supposed to be a watchdog for the stockholders whom they represent. Presumably they should object if management tries to punish the auditors for standing up for accurate reporting. At least they should have been exposed to Lybrand's side of the argument.

We had one last question for French. If Cerro had waited one more month before firing Lybrand, then all of the arguing that took place over 1971 financial statements need not have been disclosed by Lybrand in its Form 8-K letter since it would have taken place more than 18 months before. Why hadn't Cerro waited? French replied that Cerro was anxious to get under way on its 1973 audit. "We weren't going to put off the decision regarding accounting firms until we were clear of all possible disputes," he said. "That just didn't enter our thinking."

We could come to only one conclusion: That Cerro had hoped that nobody who mattered would pay attention to the Form 8-K letters. Why, we wondered, doesn't the SEC insist that these letters be mailed to stockholders and to brokerage houses?

Considering how close Cerro had come to sweeping the whole thing under the rug, it is a fair question to ask whether the whole Form 8-K procedure does any good unless it is given wide circulation. ▪

October 1, 1973

How to keep
from being taken

Nobody expects an annual report to trumpet out where management went wrong. But read those footnotes—and the phrasing of the accountant's letter. They will often tell quite a revealing story.

There is a kind of Gresham's Law in accounting whereby the bad coin drives out the good. To mix the metaphor: Permissive accounting is contagious. And during the late Sixties the contagion caught many of the sounder, conservative companies.

The course of the disease is easy to trace. First the idea is created that there are, yes there really are, earnings curves that can rise in unbroken lines. Then investors are persuaded to put a premium on such curves; and to sneer at companies whose curves run flat or follow a fluctuating course.

Those without the right kind of curve get hit where it hurts: right in their price/earnings ratios. A cyclical company, no matter how good it is, is lucky to fetch ten times earnings in the marketplace. Those with sweeping up-curves go for 20, 30, even 50 times earnings. What *that* does to stock options, merger possibilities, even to corporate prestige is all too obvious.

In the next phase of the disease, imaginative types start doing things with their books so that it looks to investors as though *they*, too, have those lovely curves even if they don't really. As the myth becomes more widely accepted and investors more uncritical, this imaginative accounting wins rich rewards for its practitioners.

In the final phase, the contagion becomes an epidemic. Even sound, businesslike managements come down with the disease. They almost have to: Their very existence is threatened by companies who know how to use high price/earnings stocks to take over low P/E companies.

What does it all add up to? It adds up to trouble. Today a majority of annual reports must be read skeptically. Many are outright deceptive. Only a minority are truly frank and honest. This, despite some 15 "Opinions" handed down by the Accounting Principles Board of the American Institute of Certified Public Accountants in the last eight years, and despite rulings promulgated by the Securities & Exchange Commission, and despite so-called full disclosure by management. The annual report has fallen to the lowest ebb of confidence it has reached in many years.

Says Thorton O'Glove, a shrewd observer who writes a monthly accounting bulletin for the brokerage firm of Scheinman, Hochstin & Trotta: "We are in an accounting recession which is feeding an earnings recession. That has led to a widespread reassessment of the price/earnings multiple of many companies." O'Glove feels that the accountants, in particular the Accounting Principles Board, have only served to widen the credibility gap with a number of obtuse and inflammatory "Opinions."

But it is quite unfair to place the blame on the accountants alone. Wall Street, in its obsession with growth in earnings per share is guilty, too. Yet Wall Street could not have gotten very far if many managements hadn't gone along with them. And the final blame must go to the investors whose greed and gullibility led them to ignore the well-documented lessons of history.

How the Growth and Performance Cult led to the Takeover Game is well known. As big companies sought ways to check the takeover boys, they began to use some of the tricks that loose accounting rules permitted. Thus in 1968 many steel companies changed from the accelerated-depreciation method of accounting to the straight-line method, which added millions of dollars to reported earnings. That was further augmented by a change to the flow-through method of accounting for the investment credit by a number of steel companies.

The financially hard-pressed airlines stretched out depreciation on their jet aircraft from 11 to 12-14 years. A number of companies have switched from last-in, first-out inventory to first-in, first-out to make reported earnings look better. All are moves away from conservatism.

This couldn't last forever, however. Many of these bookkeeping switches amounted to nothing more than borrowing from future earnings. Not surprisingly it was the earlier and wilder practioners of permissive accounting who got their comeuppance first. Taking capital gains into common share earnings did wonders for companies like National General, Northwest Industries and Gulf & Western. But capital gains transactions work both ways, and last year National General had to take a huge capital loss. Northwest has some potentially big losses should it sell out. Gulf & Western made its earnings look better by taking into earnings stock market profits. But it probably will have no such profits this current fiscal year. Add to that the fact that G&W's operating earnings are turning down, and you have the makings of a major decline in G&W's reported earnings.

Tighten the Rules

Says a Wall Street analyst who will not be named: "In the past few years a lot of these companies squeezed big mileage out of favorable accounting options. But now the same options are working *against* them."

Faced with public disillusion, law suits and with the threat of scandals yet to come, the accountants are trying to tighten the rules. For example, they propose sharply curtailing the number of cases in which "pooling" of mergers for stock will be allowed. Pooling has been very important for growth companies. It allows them to profitably combine another company's earnings, which the growth companies, because of their higher price/earnings ratio, acquired with a smaller number of shares. And in pooling, when a premium is paid over assets, no goodwill is recorded on the books.

Along with this jarring body blow, the accountants also propose to force companies making a "purchase" for cash to start writing off any new goodwill that may arise when they pay more than the acquired companies' assets are worth. Such write-offs, taken over about a period of 40 years, will penalize earnings each year. Not surprisingly, a good many merger-minded companies are protesting. One such is International Telephone & Telegraph, which counts heavily on an ever-rising earnings curve to keep its stock relatively high and to facilitate mergers; ITT is uncomfortably aware of what happened to the Litton Industries myth once its curve was broken in 1968 (Litton has dropped from $125 to under $20). Other companies whose earnings growth could be hurt by the proposed merger accounting rules change: U.S. Industries, City Investing, Whittaker Corp., Teledyne, AMK.

Already, many fast-growth companies have had their images somewhat tarnished by the rule, put into effect in 1969 by the AICPA, which requires companies to report to stockholders what the effect would be on earnings if convertible securities were actually converted.

But these new rules cover only a small percentage of the cases where confusing and sometimes misleading reporting is freely used. Once there was magic in the famous two paragraphs:

"We have examined the consolidated balance sheet of The XYZ Co. and subsidiaries as of December 31, and the related statements of income, retained earnings and capital surplus, and the statement of source and application of funds for the year then ended. Our examination was made in accordance with generally accepted auditing procedures as we considered necessary in the circumstances.

"In our opinion, the accompanying consolidated financial statements present fairly the financial position of The XYZ Co. and subsidiaries at December 31, and the results of their operations for the year then ended, in conformity with generally accepted accounting principles which have been applied on a basis consistent with that of the preceding year."

To the ordinary investor—and to many Wall Streeters—these two paragraphs signified that men of exceptional probity had checked the figures and found them sound. Then came the scandals. Yale Express. Westec. Continental Vending. The public learned that the two paragraphs, in themselves, gave no guarantee of the facts upon which the figures were supposedly based. Since then the accountants have become more careful. For those willing to make the effort, annual reports have begun to have more of a between-the-lines meaning.

There is, for example, the now fairly common phrase "subject to" in an audited statement, the "subject" usually specified in a footnote to the report. Explains New York University accounting associate professor and editor of the *ERA Accounting Review*, Lee J. Seidler: "A 'subject to' is the closest thing to a refusal of certification of a key item that an auditor can make. It means he is in serious disagreement with the company about its disclosure or lack of disclosure, concerning an important area."

A "subject to" can indicate that assets and earnings are as indicated only if inventories or other assets like investments are really worth what the company claims; this claim the auditor does not certify.

Ling-Temco-Vought's 1969 annual report is thick with "subject to's." In it, L-T-V's accountants, Ernst & Ernst, constantly qualify their certification with such phrases as the following:

"In our opinion, subject to, 1) the effect of the matter described in the preceding paragraph [divestiture of one or more subsidiaries required by the Justice Department within three years], 2) any adjustments which might be required upon settlement of the several matters as described under contingencies in Note G; and 3) the realization of the estimated future income tax benefits as explained in Note I, the accompanying financial statements . . . present fairly the respective financial positions at December 31, 1969 and the respective results of operations, changes in stockholders' equity and source and use of working capital for the year then ended, all in conformity with generally accepted accounting principles applied on a basis consistent with the preceding year, after giving effect to the restatement for debt discount as described in Note M."

What this means, bluntly, is: Here are the figures, but we won't swear by them; too many imponderables. What *were* L-T-V's earnings? Well, the company reported 1) $2.3 million in income before extraordinary items, 2) a $38.3-million loss after extraordinary items, chiefly losses on sale of investments and unprofitable operations, 3) also a $30-million reserve for possible losses on the anticipated sale of Braniff and the Okonite Co. But there was more, much more.

For one thing, L-T-V disclosed that it was considering augmenting the $30-million reserve by an additional $38 million in 1970. This extra sum would come from the adjusted book profit realized on the February 1970 sale of its 75 percent interest in Wilson Sporting Goods. Said L-T-V: "There is considerable latitude in the method and timing of the disposition of these assets and the ultimate loss, if any, cannot be determined at this time."

Profits in the Future

Another interesting footnote concerned L-T-V's Jones & Laughlin Steel subsidiary. J&L reported $22 million in profits, even though it reported a loss to the IRS. However, $13 million of that book profit was from the sale of future production of mineral deposits at a discount; in other words, J&L was taking profits now for something it would produce later on.

These are some of the "subject to's" that a single big company was involved with last year. Properly read, they can warn an investor of impending disaster. Lockheed Aircraft's 1968 report was a good example. Properly read, it gave hints of the dire reading that Lockheed's 1969 report would make a year later.

Lockheed, now in serious financial difficulties, which it only began to disclose fully in 1969 and early 1970, was slapped with a "subject-to" audit of its 1968 annual report by Arthur Young & Co. Said the accounting firm, "In our opinion, subject to the realization of the work-in-process inventories and accounts receivable described in Note 2, the statements mentioned above present fairly, . . . except for the change in accounting for administrative and general expenses and independent research and development costs described in Note 1."

The change in accounting in Note 1 increased earnings by $22 million, out of a total of $44 million reported. On top of this, Lockheed increased earnings by including an $18.7-million refund of prior years' income tax arising from loss carrybacks of previous years. Note 2 had to do with estimated costs on the C-5 aircraft. Lockheed claimed there would be no loss, but pointed out that complete realization of inventories would depend on the accuracy of estimated costs. Additionally, income recorded on long-term shipbuilding and construction contracts was based on estimates of completion cost. Initial claims aggregating $140 million for recovery were filed. The ultimate *realization* of receivables and inventories based on such estimates was dependent upon the collection of a major portion of the claims.

In other words, if Lockheed couldn't collect, it could be in for a major disaster, running into the hundreds of millions. In Lockheed's 1969 annual report, the full magnitude of the disaster started to unfold. The report took on a funereal aspect. The auditor reminded stockholders that they were still giving a major qualification regarding the realization of certain inventories and receivables.

Said Arthur Young & Co.: "As discussed in Notes 2 and 3, the company is faced with contingencies of extraordinary magnitudes arising from disputes with, and claims against, the U.S. Government as well as uncertainty as to its commercial TriStar program. These items are material to both the financial position and the results of the operations of the company, and their resolution may significantly affect its future. In our opinion, subject to the effect of the matters referred to in the preceding paragraph. . ."

In 1969 Lockheed reported a $77-million pretax loss *vs.* a 1968 profit of $44 million. Lockheed showed a $150-million provision in 1969 for losses on contracts, but in Note 2 and elsewhere it pointed out that the ultimate loss on various government contracts could total as much as $500 million before income-tax effect.

So much for the "real" value of Lockheed's inventory in 1968's report.

Don't think that you can skip the footnotes just because the company receives no accountants' objection.

The Boeing Co. audit by Touche Ross & Co. contained no "subject to's" or "except for's." The footnotes, nevertheless, were well worth reading.

One footnote for 1969 pointed out that Boeing's pension costs rose sharply last year; however, the charge for pensions against 1969 earnings declined. The reason: Boeing, by making higher pension actuarial assumptions, was able to make up the difference. Still, the fact remained: Pension costs for 1969 were higher than pension charges for 1968, and future earnings will be affected. It also reported a $10-million net profit, but that was only after tax credits of $25 million.

Properly understanding an airline's annual report requires considerable patience. Pan American World Airways confessed in its annual report to a loss of $26 million (*vs.* a profit of $49 million for 1968). But the loss would have been greater had Pan Am not capitalized some interest charges ($16 million) and had it not reduced pension charges by reducing reserves ($3.5 million).

If there were a prize for the annual report that goes furthest in trying to put a good face on a bad situation, that prize would go to Penn Central. The company had a simply disastrous year in 1969. Nevertheless, it managed to report a small ($4-million) net profit before an extraordinary loss of $125 million. It did so by imaginative bookkeeping and tax offsets.

Some of Penn Central's losses were debited to a reserve set up some years before—instead of being charged to earnings. Others were offset by reduced depreciation charges—which were probably already inadequate to replacement costs—and by reducing freight and car rental expenses by $7 million retroactively. While consolidating every item it could find to improve the profit, Penn Central conveniently *avoids* consolidating the $6-million loss suffered by the Lehigh Valley. Yet it took in $9 million in Wabash dividends—also not consolidated.

Significant sidelight: In its report to the Interstate Commerce Commission, which is not interested in so-called accounting principles, Penn Central showed a

$22-million greater loss on its railroad operations than the $56-million loss it showed for the railroad company.

Continuing on its merry way in the first quarter of 1970 PC reported a $17-million loss. But that was only after a $51-million capital gain from the sale of its Wabash investment and an intercompany transaction of dubious nature.

Sometimes the only way to understand a company's annual report is to compare it with another report in the same general line of business. For example, Control Data's 1969 annual report makes more sense when read in conjunction with that of IBM.

Last year Control Data resorted to a number of devices that significantly aided earnings, including 1) sale of lease rights for $39 million, 2) deferred research and development costs and other deferred charges of $28 million that found their way onto the balance sheet. This has the effect of reducing current charges, 3) a capital gain of $2.6 million. On the other hand, IBM expenses such items or doesn't utilize such devices.

These intercompany comparisons are especially interesting among financial firms. Operating almost side-by-side in the insurance business out of Hartford, Conn., The Travelers and Aetna Life & Casualty present some interesting bookkeeping contrasts. Last year Aetna reported a sharp decline in earnings while Travelers had a sharp gain. A careful comparison of the companies' 1969 reports suggests the reason: While both companies were hit by heavy losses in their underwriting businesses last year, Travelers had more nearly provided for the losses by setting aside adequate reserves in earlier years, while Aetna had not.

In another sense, however, Travelers was more conservative than Aetna. Travelers had been expensing certain costs in the issuance of new individual life insurance policies, now it is accruing them like everyone else. This jumped reported 1969 earnings by well over 20 percent.

If you want to be thoroughly confused, try analyzing bank annual reports. Under pressure from analysts and accountants, the banks finally agreed to debit earnings by any gains or losses in the bond market (previously these were charged to special reserves or capital accounts).

The consequence has been that many banks reported a noticeably lower net income figure after security losses. Worse still, it appears that for at least 1970, using the existing formula, earnings would be depressed even more.

This hasn't made the bankers very happy and a number of them, including the president of First National City Bank, Walter Wriston, are urging a change or a return to the old method. They say that the new one is more distorting than the old one. Accountants like Leonard Savoie of the AICPA say the banks are throwing up a red herring, since a banker's committee had agreed to the new system. Which suggests that nobody really knows the true profit figure.

Many more conservative companies in the last few years, under pressure, have tried to put a better face on earnings, although they haven't been quite as blatant as some of the conglomerates that have tried to take them over. For example, International Harvester, like everybody else, has been having earnings problems. It decided to do what many steel companies had done in 1968. It changed its depreciation accounting, thus adding some $7.2 million to 1969's anemic income. IH, in the prior year, had already changed the allocation of taxes in such a way as to benefit reported short-term earnings. The effect was to increase earnings in 1969 by $5.8 million and in 1968 by $6.8 million.

Still Pitching

To some, it appeared that the steel companies had pretty much exhausted their accounting options in 1968 when they added around $100 million to their income statements by changing from accelerated depreciation to straight-line depreciation. But a look at the 1969 annual reports of Bethlehem Steel and U.S. Steel indicates that they are still in there pitching.

It turns out that both Bethlehem & U.S. Steel in the last few years have been selling future mineral production payments running into several hundred million dollars. While they don't take profits on the sale into earnings immediately, they do take some of it into the next year's earnings by a reduction of taxes. They don't disclose how much. For another, until last year this enabled them to get reductions in current income taxes but now the law has been changed.

Nonetheless, both companies have a very low income tax rate for this and several other reasons. For example, Bethlehem Steel last year paid only $33 million in income taxes on pretax net of $189 million. This was possible, in part, by a $32-million investment tax credit offset.

U.S. Steel paid only $68 million in income taxes on $285 million in pretax net for many of the same reasons. Big Steel also changed actuarial assumptions on its pension funds, thus saving more than $14 million after taxes in 1969. Bethlehem also changed pension accounting late last year, but it had a small impact on earnings. Finally, U.S. Steel, by an indirect method, took into income $8 million from the sale of a plant.

This does not suggest that every company is prettifying its books. There are still many companies, Union Pacific, du Pont, Eastman Kodak, IBM, Corning Glass among them, that lean over backward to keep conservative books. Not so long ago, this looked like fuddy-duddyism, but no longer. Investors are learning once again the meaning of the old phrase "the quality of earnings." In short, they are learning that simply because two companies each report earnings of $2 a share, it does not mean that both of them are equally profitable. On a strictly comparable basis, one of them might only be earning $1.50 a share and the other closer to $2.50. High-quality earnings also are more stable earnings: By borrowing, in effect, from the future the less conservative companies run the risk of a severe down-turn when business weakens; the more conservative companies, by contrast, have a kind of built-in stabilizer.

Realizing this, investors have begun to shift their investing habits. Old-line companies, once scorned for their flat earnings curves, are coming back in favor: It's no accident that du Pont has been one of the stronger market performers this year. On the other hand, conglomerates, whose bookkeeping is especially suspect, have had their price/earnings ratios cut to pieces. And, realizing that many fancier-looking earnings curves are subject to manipulation, the market has been marking down many companies with a high P/E ratio.

But then maybe investors—not to mention businessmen who bought companies on the basis of embellished figures—should have paid more attention to the footnotes and the accounting changes in the first place. ■

May 15, 1970

8

CONCLUSION

We kicked off *Forbes Numbers Game* with "That's a lot of GAAP!"—an irreverent piece that questioned the value of accounting's fundamental body of concepts and rules, Generally Accepted Accounting Principles, or GAAP. That article and many that followed it came down pretty hard on the accounting profession. Have we been unjustly unsympathetic? Perhaps. As we stressed at the outset, few areas of accounting today present easy *questions* let alone clear-cut answers. This basic fact is the burden of *Forbes Numbers Game's* two concluding articles.

The first piece tackles two fundamental questions: For whom—lawyers? managements? investors? bankers?—do accountants work? and, Who should write accounting rules? Private sector accountants? Or the government? The article argues, in effect, that while the accounting rules (and rule-writers) we've got are far from perfect, they are far superior to the rules we've had—and to the politician rule-writers we might have. The second article, "So whaddya suggest?" suggests that like our national politicians, our leading businessmen, critics of accounting offer little in the way of constructive criticism.

Should accounting principles be set in Washington, D.C. by politicians and career bureaucrats?

Or should Big (and little) Business have more influence on accounting principles and rules than they now have?

Or is the *status quo* the best we can hope for?

The only certain thing is that you'll hear these questions debated increasingly and with accumulating intensity in the years ahead. Which side is right? This particular accounting judgment we leave to you. We leave you it

157

along with Ohio State Professor John Shank's maxim: "No matter how detailed the accounting rules, the mind of the enterprising entrepreneur can always conceive of a transaction consistent with the rules but inconsistent with the spirit behind them." Whoever writes the accounting rules will do well to keep this rather depressing but certainly true thought in mind.

Why everybody's jumping on the accountants these days

Whom do the accountants work for? Their clients? Investors? Or for Ralph Nader and the federal government? That's one of the vital issues at stake in the current bitter hassle over accounting and auditing.

Lee Seidler, now a professor at New York University and a consultant at Bear, Stearns & Co., tells a revealing story about the limitations of the accounting profession.

"I used to work on the audit of a major motion picture company," says Seidler, 42.' One of the key valuation problems was films that had been recently released. Unreleased films were valued at cost, so they were no problem. But some films had been released at the year's end and had gotten poor reviews. The question was, should we write them down or not?

"We had a minimal amount of objective evidence. Just a couple of bad reviews and a few weeks of audience figures. But there was a guy there who did their internal projections of how the films would do. He'd say, for instance, 'This film will do well in Europe; don't worry that it's doing poorly in the U.S.' He was usually right. We relied on him, discovering over the years that he was about as accurate a source as could be found." What more, Seidler wonders, could any auditor do in that situation? Auditors, after all, are not film critics.

But to do the job that some people expect of them, auditors would have to be much more than just film critics. To run down all corporate misbehavior, they would have to be detectives. To certify a client's conformity with regulations such as antitrust and environmental laws, they would have to be legal experts.

On top of all this, the accounting profession's critics have one more small request: They want a system of accounting that is as useful to government policymakers, consumers and other groups as it is to investors and creditors.

The prospect—some would say the certainty—of change, drastic change, is very much in the air right now for the accounting profession. Everyone wants to see financial accounting get closer to the truth—and everyone has his own idea of what "the truth" is. Many people would like to require the accountants to be watchdogs of public and business morality. Pressure on the accountants is intense. Most of it is coming, not from business itself, but from politicians. Accounting might seem a strange issue for a shrewd politician to grab hold of, but these particular ones know very well what they are doing. The principal activists in Congress are Senator William Proxmire (D-Wis.), Senator Lee Metcalf (D-Mont.) and Representative John Moss (D-Cal.)

Proxmire is upset because established accounting did not lead to exposure of illegal bribes by business. Moss is concerned about the same problem. He is particularly incensed about the diversity of accounting practices in the oil and gas industry. The most vehement of the three is Metcalf, who has long maintained that electric utility accounting constitutes a ripoff of the consumer. If Metcalf has his way, accounting standards will be legislated by a federal agency—the way meat standards or drug standards are.

The Securities & Exchange Commission is also pushing for change, although of a less drastic kind: The SEC wants accountants to be tougher with their clients, but is willing to let the accountants themselves set the standards. Meanwhile, the accountants are trying to head the Feds off at the pass by tightening the rules themselves.

Can you treat accounting figures like meat or pharmaceuticals? Should the federal government, acting on behalf not only of stockholders and creditors but of the general public as well, force its own accounting standards on business?

This much is certain: There have been serious abuses in business and accounting in the past. Problems began to mount in the twilight of the go-go 1960s when a rash of notorious bankruptcies and frauds shook the public's confidence in certified public accountancy: Penn Central, National Student Marketing, Equity Funding, Stirling Homex. The accounting profession's rules clearly failed to deal with earnings manipulation and corporate hanky-panky. The SEC came down hard on the CPAs, as did the courts, which were flooded with litigation from angry investors.

The latest in a series of blows to the profession came three months ago, from a subcommittee headed by Senator Lee Metcalf. It was in the form of a blistering, 1,760-page staff report calling for a government takeover of accounting rules and auditing standards. The report also demanded greater responsibility by CPAs for detecting and disclosing illegal acts by their clients.

Belatedly the profession is making its own efforts to put its house in order. A Commission on Auditors' Responsibilities appointed 2-1/2 years ago by the CPA's professional association, the American Institute of Certified Public Accountants, is expected to call shortly for wide-ranging reforms in auditing practices and standards. Among other things, the AICPA's commission will propose that auditors narrow management's traditionally wide discretion to choose alternate accounting methods.

At the same time, the profession is trying to hammer out a better system of producing accounting principles. The Financial Accounting Standards Board, established in 1973 by the AICPA and four other professional groups to set all accounting principles, is due for some organizational changes. The changes, expected soon, are aimed at speeding up the FASB's cumbersome pace—which some critics say involves excessive attention to "due process."

The FASB itself is working on a "conceptual framework" of accounting— sort of an accounting constitution. Among the questions: What exactly *are* earnings? What is an asset? A liability? How should assets be measured—by their historical cost, as they are presently? Or by some measure of current value? In short, do present financial statements reflect reality? Or just an arbitrary semblance of reality?

Such reforms, however, are unlikely to end the matter. The confrontation between the accounting profession and its critics has two distinct but related rounds: Round One is over accounting principles—the rules specifying acceptable methods of measuring company finances. Round Two is over auditing standards and responsibilities—the regulations governing CPA duties in auditing clients' books.

Who Shall Set
Accounting Principles?

The Metcalf report charges that private bodies that set accounting stan- dards—the FASB and its predecessor, the Accounting Principles Board—have kowtowed to the wishes of the "Big Eight" accounting firms.* According to the report, the Big Eight identify their interests with their biggest corporate clients and therefore influence the FASB to produce lax, namby-pamby principles.

What is the SEC supposed to be doing while all of this is going on? Ac- cording to the report, the SEC started the whole charade by delegating its authority over accounting principles back in 1938. Of the FASB, the report says: "During its three-year existence, none of [the FASB's standards] has seriously threatened the accounting prerogatives of various special-interest groups in the established business community." The whole report might have been written by William Jennings Bryan. Its old-fashioned populist premise is that businessmen are rogues and guilty until proved innocent. It's as ridiculous in its way as the old-fashioned businessman's attitude that what he does is no- body's business but his own.

If most corporate executives have long since abandoned this attitude, a good many nevertheless think the accountants are looking for a degree of pure, untarnished truth that doesn't reflect the real world of business. They point,

*Price Waterhouse & Co.; Arthur Andersen & Co.; Coopers & Lybrand; Haskins & Sells; Peat Marwick Mitchell & Co.; Arthur Young & Co.; Ernst & Ernst; Touche Ross & Co.

for instance, to the FASB's controversial Statement 8, which required companies to show the effect of foreign currency fluctuations on their quarterly earnings statements. The way the corporations see it, currency movements have little to do with earnings performance overseas. Philip Morris was so incensed over this ruling that it refused to publicly restate its 1975 earnings to compare with 1976's, saying the comparison would show an "artificial" rise in profit.

So, there you have the impasse. It is as though everybody was speaking a different language: most businessmen feeling that the accountants have already gone to ridiculous extremes to assure "realistic" accounting; activist politicians accusing the accountants and businessmen of being in bed together; and the accountants getting it from both sides.

Who is right? Everybody is and nobody is. The fact is that accounting is an art, a set of conventions developed over time; not a science, a set of laws verified in a laboratory. So the best we can do is ask: What is the *most* meaningful Accounting Truth?

Take FASB Statement 8. Corporate executives think it only confuses investors to allow currency fluctuations to cause swings in earnings from period to period. But the FASB ruled that currency fluctuations are part of today's economic reality, so they should be reflected immediately. Who is *right*? Both parties are. But it makes a big difference *which* truth is chosen.

Or take the FASB's Statement 2, which requires companies to deduct research and development expenditures from income in the period in which they are made. Some argue that research and development costs are investments for the future, the same as a new plant, and ought to be capitalized as assets and written down over a period of time. But the FASB ruled that they should be expensed immediately, because their future value is too subjective to judge reliably.

"Reality" and "truth" are only part of the dilemma. Listen to John C. (Sandy) Burton, New York's deputy mayor for finance and former chief accountant of the Securities & Exchange Commission: "The way you keep score determines at least in part the way you play the game." Burton means that if you drastically change the way businesses keep their books, you inevitably change some of the ways in which they are run.

Of course, this isn't the way it *should* be. Ideally, accounting should simply abstract the situation, describe it in numbers. But everybody knows that pooling-of-interest accounting, which tends to inflate reported earnings after a merger, helped encourage the conglomerate craze of the late Sixties, and that changing those rules made conglomeration much less attractive. This is only one example of how managements are frequently encouraged—or even forced—to make business decisions whose only purpose is to make the numbers look good, irrespective of the long-range impact. Consider two others: FASB Statement 8, say big multinationals, necessitates inefficient currency hedging to dampen earnings fluctuations. FASB Statement 2, say little growth firms, discourages research and development.

Change the accounting rules drastically and most corporate earnings as we now know them could disappear. Change them in yet another way and book value, the asset value, of many stocks could double or even treble. In either case, managements of many publicly owned corporations, concerned over the stock market impact, would probably run their businesses differently.

"It's hard to tell in advance what effect a principle will have," says the FASB's scholarly vice chairman, Robert Sprouse, a former Stanford University professor. "But once we make our best judgment, we have to weigh the possible costs to society against the benefits." That's right, costs and benefits: They have a place in accounting too. That is, the benefit to the capital market of improved financial information must be weighed against the cost of any changes in economic behavior induced by new accounting rules. Says Sandy Burton: "There is no doubt that measurement standards have an impact on behavior. That impact cannot be ignored in setting measurement standards. There's a delicate balance you have to have."

Delicate balances, of course, lead to messy, imperfect compromises. An example is the FASB's recent Statement 13 on accounting for leases. The FASB heard anguished pleas from some companies that their bond indentures would be technically abrogated if they were forced to capitalize leases on their balance sheets as liabilities. The board reluctantly agreed that would be true in some cases. Says Sprouse: "To take overnight action could throw things in an uproar. With publicly held debt obligations, you might have to get a vote of all the bondholders around the country to get approval of a change in the indenture." Accordingly, the board provided a four-year grace period for firms to change over; after 1980, nearly all leases must be capitalized.

That's a pretty messy compromise—albeit a necessary one. But the accountants say it's nothing compared with the mess that would occur if the numbers they assemble were used as instruments of public policy. "It would be a great mistake," says Burton, "if standard-setting bodies were to start establishing standards *because* of the economic effect they have." But that's exactly what would happen, warn the accountants, if the government set accounting principles.

In 1971, for example, the now-defunct Accounting Principles Board, in the interest of conservative financial reporting, stated that the investment tax credit should be amortized over the life of the asset for which it applies. Congress, however, had a different idea: It wanted the credit to give a quick boost to corporate profits. Consequently, it passed a law prohibiting auditors from prescribing any particular accounting treatment of the credit—thereby allowing companies to flow the credit through to earnings all at once or amortize it as they pleased. That may have been good economic policy, but it hardly promoted uniform accounting standards.

There are plenty of other cases where politicians have dabbled in accounting issues. Senator Metcalf's interest in changing electric utility accounting for consumers' benefit is one example. Another is Congressman William Hughes (D-N.J.), who maintains that oil and gas companies use accounting gimmickry to "hide profits" from the public. Whether or not they're right is not at issue here. The point is: Financial statements cannot be all things to all people. What one man sees as "hidden profit" may be what another views as conservative accounting practice.

So what *should* financial statements be? The FASB has proposed an answer to that question as part of its "conceptual framework" project. According to the FASB, financial statements should "provide information that helps investors and creditors assess the prospects of receiving cash from dividends or interest, and from proceeds from the sale, redemption or maturity of securities or loans."

This is no empty platitude. Its emphasis on aiding investors and creditors could involve conflicts with other goals—such as aiding Washington's economic policy, or encouraging more research and development, or unveiling the oil companies' hidden "obscene" profits for every angry consumer to behold. These other goals can't be ignored, but the FASB seems to believe—quite properly—that they must take a back seat to the primary goal of serving the capital market.

Does this mean that stockholders and bankers are more "important" than ordinary people? Not at all. But the capital market is the means by which society allocates its resources; its information system can be muddied or distorted by political considerations only at some peril.

What Audit Standard—And For Whom?

All this comes under the heading of accounting principles—the rules for preparing financial statements. There is also the matter of *auditing standards*—the rules for validating the numbers that go into the books. Here, too, the Metcalf report demands a new tangle of federal regulation to sort things out. The report recommends that the federal government itself take over the setting and monitoring of auditing standards, and that auditors be held liable for simple negligence in failing to detect fraud and illegal acts by clients. Because auditors can't be trusted to maintain an arms-length relationship with clients, Metcalf suggests that Congress consider a Ralph Nader-backed proposal that would require all companies to rotate auditing firms at least once very few years. The report also suggests that the Federal Trade Commission and U.S. Justice Department investigate the Big Eight accounting firms to see if their size and market share violate antitrust laws.

There are some very basic issues involved here—which the Metcalf report simply ignores. The fact is that requiring *too* much of the auditors will involve great cost to society. The auditing fees of the Big Eight firms alone already add up to well over $1 billion annually, and that's just for sampling parts of the corporate books. "If we insist that auditors explore every nook and cranny of every company they audit, the cost will be astronomical," says Philip Defliese, senior partner of Coopers & Lybrand.

As things are now, it already takes huge firms with great resources to audit the world's multinational corporations effectively. "What really kills me," says Russell Palmer, managing partner of Touche Ross & Co., "is when you get these guys saying that the Big Eight are too big. But then we're condemned because we missed some illegal payment in Milan before anyone knew there was an illegal payments problem. Come on!"

It also takes a big firm to be able to stand up to the corporations when disputes arise in the course of an audit. If a firm doesn't have a large number of big corporate accounts, it is more likely to buckle when a big client wants to do things its own way.

Rotating auditing firms, moreover, has its drawbacks. It takes a great deal of knowledge about a company to perform an effective audit. In fact, many of the auditing failures of the past decade occurred because the auditors were new to the companies or industries they were auditing—not because they had become "cozy" with them. "Almost all of the problem cases occurred in the first- or second-year audits of the client," says New York University's Lee Seidler. "For the most part, audit busts have not occurred in cases where accounting firms had audited clients for ten years. They've occurred right in the beginning." The Penn Central debacle, for instance, occurred in the first year that PC was audited by Peat Marwick. This is one reason why rotating auditors to insure "independence" may not work.

Does all this mean that we can't improve on the status quo? That we can't heap greater responsibility for fairer financial reporting on the auditing profession? That we can't keep auditors constantly on the lookout for management misbehavior without imparing their ability to work? Not at all.

One of the most promising areas for improvement is that of making sure that alternative practices available under Generally Accepted Accounting Principles no longer cloak "creative accounting" techniques. In the late Sixties and early Seventies, investors learned the hard way that an ingenious concoction of GAAPs may not "fairly present" at all. Thus, the SEC in September 1975 issued Accounting Series Release 177, which required companies changing from one GAAP to another to present a letter from their auditors confirming that the change was to a *preferable* method under the circumstances—and explaining why.

Suppose, for instance, that Whoopee Industries, Inc. wants to change from the highflyer method of accounting for its widget operations to the conservative method. Under ASR 177, Whoopee would have to submit a letter from its auditors explaining whether or not the conservative method was preferable in Whoopee's circumstances.

The ruling was not well received initially by the CPAs, although most of them are slowly accepting it. A major exception is Big Eight firm Arthur Andersen & Co., ever the outspoken maverick of the accounting world. Andersen filed suit against the SEC over the issue, horrifying the rest of the profession—which fears that parts of the suit threaten to turn accounting principles over to the government.

But Harvey Kapnick, Andersen's chairman and chief executive, insists that he hardly wants anything like that to happen. "The question of preferability," Kapnick told FORBES, "is really a matter of frustration over how to get to uniform accounting. And how are you going to get to uniformity?" According to Kapnick, the FASB or APB should have devised a system of consistent accounting principles long ago. But alas, they haven't. So, Kapnick asks: "Should the individual auditor, acting on his own, decide these questions?"

Against Kapnick's judgment, the answer to that question will be "yes"—at least, if the AICPA's Commission on Auditors' Responsibilities has its way. The commission will recommend that, except in a very small number of toss-up cases, management will not have a free chioce among various Generally Accepted Accounting Pinciples. The auditors will have to decide which method they consider preferable in each client's case.

Go back to the example of Whoopee Industries. Under the AICPA commission's proposal, Whoopee's auditors would have to *insist* that the company change from the highflyer method to the conservative method, if they believed the conservative method preferable in Whoopee's case. If Whoopee refused, the auditors would have to qualify their report.

Is it unreasonable to ask auditors to assume this responsibility? Kapnick clearly thinks so, but Sandy Burton says pointedly: "I've never yet seen a situation where a client came to an accountant and asked: 'How shall we account for this?'—and the accountant hasn't been able to come up with something he'd recommend."

The AICPA's commission is also coming out with recommendations on auditors' responsibilities for dealing with management fraud and illegal acts. Says Lee Seidler, who served as deputy chairman of the commission: "Believe it or not, some accountants say that they're not supposed to hunt for fraud. We think the auditor is kidding himself if he believes that. On the other hand, we think the public ought to realize that the auditor is not very good at *finding* it, because there is usually a deliberate attempt to hide it from him. People tend to think of auditors as detectives. They're not—they're accountants. We train them in debits and credits. Even if they look carefully, auditors will miss many, maybe even most, frauds."

Similarly, Seidler continues, the problem with exposing illegal corporate acts is that auditors aren't supermen. Any company these days is bound to be on the borderline of violating some antitrust statute, some environmental regulation, or some other law. If auditors *do* find clear instances of payoffs to government officials, or violations of other regulations, they should report them to the board of directors' audit committee and see that proper action is taken—that, Seidler says, is their duty. But it would be silly to expect accountants to be society's experts on fine points of law and morality.

What it all boils down to is this: The accountants failed to prevent the corporate abuses that were so common in the late 60s and early 70s. They paid a high price in the courts—as well as in loss of professional esteem. Since then, however, they have cleaned up their acts considerably, and appear to be well on the way to appreciating the extent of their responsibilities to the capital market—and the corresponding responsibility to stand up to their clients.

It would be a bad thing for everybody if, in punishing the accountants for sins now atoned for, the politicians were to subvert the true (if somewhat limited) function of certified public accounting—and at the same time foist upon this country yet another maze of regulations, yet more miles of costly red tape. ■

March 15, 1977

EPILOGUE: Senator Lee Metcalf died unexpectedly on January 12, 1978, only a few months after his Subcommittee On Reports, Accounting and Management issued its enormous staff study, *The Accounting Establishment.* As expected, the subcommittee's work threw most of the accounting profession into a near-panic. Following public hearings, the Metcalf subcommittee ultimately issued a much milder report—many of the recommendations of which were previously included in the AICPA Report of the Commission on Auditors Responsibilities (the Cohen Commission.)

Metcalf's subcommittee chairmanship was assumed by Missouri Senator Thomas F. Eagleton. Eagleton may have signalled that the government's pressure on the accountants will subside further under his chairmanship when he told a group of CPAs on the first anniversary of *The Accounting Establishment*'s publication, "To be sure, much remains to be done in living up to the subcommittee's recommendations. Nevertheless, I believe the FASB is off to an impressive start." (Representative John Moss' proposed accounting legislation has so far met with scant support.)

Perhaps Senator Eagleton understands better than most American politicians—and better than the leading American businessmen featured in our following and final "Number Game"—that accounting's easy successes are behind us and that the problems remaining are hideously complex and perhaps even intractible.

So waddya suggest?

In which some of America's top executives criticize the accounting rules but fail to suggest workable alternatives.

The Financial Accounting Standards Board, scourge of flaky balance sheets and managed earnings—and, on occasion, of common sense—dwells beneath royal maples and giant black oaks in a southeastern Connecticut corporate head-quarters park just off the winding Merritt Parkway. The FASB's 106 full-time staffers and board members share their ground with geese, squirrels and such illustrous co-tenants of the glass-and-sculptured-cement building as division staffs of General Electric and Gulf & Western. It is an appropriately relaxed setting for pondering the deep-seated problems facing a profession under constant pressure to make its numbers reflect more accurately and honestly an economic reality that grows constantly more complex.

Only last month FORBES was witness to a fascinating but, alas, inconclusive confrontation in these bucolic headquarters. At the FASB's invitation, an elite group of America's most powerful businessmen assembled to confab with the board members. The businessmen were: General Motors Chairman Thomas Murphy, Du Pont Chairman Irving Shapiro, International Paper Chairman J. Stanford Smith, and AT&T Vice Chairman William Cashell. These four represent over $131 billion in corporate assets.

Since 1973, when it replaced the faction-ridden Accounting Principles Board, the FASB has turned off and teed off plenty of executives. FASB Statement No. 13, published in 1976, ended a great deal of off-blance-sheet debt financing (shrewdly used by the likes of the late W.T. Grant Co.) by forcing companies to capitalize leases. Statement 2 (issued in 1974) required companies to charge research and development costs against income, and so made it much more difficult for hot technology companies to maximize reported earnings by capitalizing their "research" program costs. Not that the FASB hasn't blown a

168

few, too. Statement 19 would have cut many smaller oil and gas companies' profits needlessly; the Security & Exchange Commission eventually scrapped the rule. The FASB's Opinion 8, whose ignorance of economic reality cut some $500 million from Royal Dutch Shell's profits last year, earned the FASB a 1977 FORBES Dubious Achievement Award.

The confrontation began at 9:30 a.m. sharp in a softly lit, heavily carpeted orange, royal blue and mocha boardroom. Oval table center stage. Curvilinear raised rows for spectators (18 men, one woman) downstate. It started with the usual pleasantries. Awfully glad you're here—We're glad to be here—We *need* your feedback—We're pleased to interface with you. And so on.

Eventually, GM Chairman Tom Murphy, a muscular-looking 44-long, led with a punch:

"The frustrating thing from our standpoint, Don [Donald Kirk, the FASB chairman], is when our financial people come in saying: 'Because of FASB Statement such and such, our financial results will change substantially.' That's a *surprise* to us and we get mad. We don't like doing something sensible and doing it consistently and suddenly having a third party come along and say. 'Do it differently.' We feel financial reporting should be *adaptive*."

In essence Murphy was saying that, since GM and other blue-chip companies follow decent, conservative accounting principles to begin with, they should not be saddled with inflexible accounting rules capable of "surprising" management and shareholders. Let accounting principles bend to fit business and not vice versa.

Had the FASB's Kirk stopped patiently chewing his eyeglass stems and pressed Murphy on the point, Murphy would have been left defending the rather untenable position that there should be one set of accounting principles for big solid companies like his and another set for weak, flaky ones.

But Kirk didn't press Murphy on this. Even when du Pont's raspy-voiced Shapiro boasted of du Pont's "gold-plated [financial] numbers" and drew on the authority of "that great American, Bert Lance" (*i.e.*, Lance's famous: "If it ain't broke, don't fix it.") Kirk kept chewing his stems.

You might think top businessmen move immediately from fuzzy theory to practical, concrete examples. Not so. The meeting—not much of a confrontation so far—was well under way before International Paper's bullnecked Chairman J. Stanford Smith brought the conservation to specifics. "The *worst* [accounting] deception," Smith said, "is trying to make things look alike that aren't alike [and vice versa] . . . For example, if your company self-insures, you cannot expense that insurance. But if we go out and *buy* insurance, then we *can* expense it. That strikes me as ludicrous."

Ah, yes. The old (but apparently ongoing) debate over FASB Statement No. 5. Statement 5 forbids managements to accrue "contingency (or catastrophe) reserve" expenses to shield earnings from real world events—a major fire, say, or lawsuit, or loss of an important customer. When it was finalized in 1975, Statement 5 was hailed by many as a major victory for sound accounting.

Yet the chairman of International Paper was taking issue with it? Indeed he was—and not alone.

Murphy: "Yeah, I have a note from Walter [Wriston, chairman of Citicorp] on that, too."

Shapiro: "What is the evil you're trying to correct [with Statement 5]? Du Pont self-insured for many years and saved stockholders a lot of money. I suppose we did smooth earnings with the [self-insurance] reserve. But we can do that if we go out and purchase insurance, too. So smoothing earnings cannot be the evil," Shapiro went on to say that as long as a company *discloses* whether it self-insures or purchases insurance, then shareholders or potential shareholders can decide for themselves if the insurance protection is adequate.

Here Kirk *did* put down his eyeglasses: "I think, Irving, that there is a fundamental concern that *somehow* disclosure is not enough."

Murphy (tensing and getting temporarily aggressive): "*Who's* concerned about that, Don?"

Kirk (soothingly but standing his ground): "It goes back to the belief of many investors that you're fooling somebody [unless] you put things into your earnings. As long as people believe that, people will suspect you."

It was at this point that the meeting verged on serious debate. One outspoken FASB board member, courtly, spectacled Robert Sprouse, tore into business' argument and vigorously defended the FASB's Statement 5:

"When you gentlemen talk about providing for protection against exposure [to catastrophes]," Sprouse demanded, "do you *really* mean a bookkeeper can debit 'insurance expense' and credit 'self-insurance reserve' and that you have then provided for protection against catastrophes? It makes no sense. Obviously you have *not* provided against catastrophes."

Sprouse meant that mere bookkeeping entries do not produce the hard cash to rebuild a burned-out plant; only a genuine insurance policy or an actual cash reserve would do that. And if earnings slump, so what? In the real world earnings *don't* climb smoothly. Surprise is in the nature of the game.

The businessmen ran for cover. "Disclosure" is the answer, was Murphy's retort. "Judgment," chimed in Shapiro, trying to change the subject.

It was time for coffee.

The businessmen returned from coffee to discuss FASB Statement 8, that patently ridiculous FASB rule under which, for example, profits of U.S. companies with assets in strong-currency countries are often marked down while profits of firms with assets in weak-currency nations are often marked up. Here, we thought, was a perfect scoring opportunity for the limping businessmen.

But the businessmen let the opportunity pass. About all that GM's Murphy could muster was to tell the FASB that Statement 8 has forced many American multinational companies to change the way they run their overseas operations.

"That disturbs me, Don." said Murphy. "It shouldn't be the thrust of accounting statements to force changes in a firm's operating practices."

Which again forced Kirk to lower his glasses and point out the obvious dilemma: "I agree, Tom. But should we promulgate accounting rules on the basis of *avoiding* changes in business behavior?"

No meaningful response.

Eventually the topic turned to inflation. The businessmen said they don't like it. And they don't like the cumbersome replacement cost information now required by the SEC to be disclosed in firms' annual reports either. Unfortunately, however, the businessmen could offer no helpful suggestions for ways in which the FASB might deal more satisfactorily with the problem.

At 12 noon sharp, the powwow was over and the businessmen headed for lunch or their limousines. FORBES cornered GM's Murphy, who reluctantly shook our hand. What, we asked him, had been the message the businessmen tried to impart to the accountants? Murphy replied:

"Er . . . no real message. We just wanted an interchange of viewpoints. We wanted to hear different viewpoints. Now if you'll excuse me . . . "

As Murphy edged away, we were left with the depressing conclusion that while there was much to criticize in the way the accountants have formulated the rules, our top businessmen have discouragingly little to recommend by way of alternatives. ■

October 13, 1978

Index

657
M 663

116 072